PAUL TILLICH

What Is Religion?

EDITED AND WITH AN INTRODUCTION BY

JAMES LUTHER ADAMS

HARPER TORCHBOOKS
Harper & Row, Publishers
New York, Hagerstown, San Francisco, London

This book was originally published in hardcover by
Harper & Row, Publishers, Inc.

The chapter *The Philosophy of Religion* was originally published under the
title *Religionsphilosophie* by Paul Tillich, by Verlag Ullstein GmbH, Frank-
furt/Main, Berlin.
The chapters *The Conquest of the Concept of Religion in the Philosophy of
Religion* and *On the Idea of a Theology of Culture* are from *Gesammelte
Werke* by Paul Tillich, originally published by Evangelisches Verlagswerk,
Stuttgart.

First HARPER TORCHBOOK edition published 1973.

STANDARD BOOK NUMBER: 06-131732-2
76 77 78 79 80   12 11 10 9 8 7 6 5 4 3

Contents

CONTENTS

Introduction

BY JAMES LUTHER ADAMS

"What do you think an artist is? A fool who, if he is a painter, has only eyes, if he is a musician, only ears, if he is a poet, only a lyre for all the chords of the heart, or even, if he is a boxer, only muscle? On the contrary, he is at the same time a social creature, always wide-awake in the face of heart-rending bitter or sweet events of the world and wholly fashioned himself according to their image. How could he fail to take an interest in other people and by virtue of what ivory-tower indifference could he detach himself from the pulsating life they bring near him? No, painting is not made to decorate houses. It is a weapon of offensive and defensive war against the enemy."

These words of Pablo Picasso are eminently pertinent at the beginning of this Introduction to a volume containing three essays by Paul Tillich on the philosophy of religion, essays that first appeared around fifty years ago. The leading essay in this volume was first published in an erudite *Handbook of Philosophy* (1925), a massive work on the academic disciplines. When it was reprinted a decade ago in the first volume of Tillich's collected writings, he spoke of it as "the first outline" of his philosophy of religion, now "recovered from the grave in which it was hidden."

9

The other two essays of the present volume were presented in 1919 and 1922 at meetings of a learned society, the Kant-Gesellschaft. Accordingly, the style of these essays is compact and abstract, and much of the language is technical. This style and this language could give the reader the false impression that the essays reflect an "ivory-tower indifference," a distance and detachment from "pulsating life."

Actually, however, these essays cannot be properly understood or appreciated if one does not bear in mind that they were composed in the turbulent years in Germany which followed World War I, a period in which cynicism, despair, radical reconception, revolutionary impulse and heady utopianism vied with each other in appeal for public favor. During these years Tillich was engaged in dialogue with a prodigious variety of people and movements. He was writing on the economic and political crisis, on socialism as a question for the church, on religion and class struggle, on "the masses and religion," on religion and art, on the youth movement, on the methods of the sciences, on nonecclesiastical religions, on special theological problems in debate, on nationalism, on the demonic in religion and culture, on the religious crisis, and on *Kairos* as a summons to new decision. Already in 1919 Karl Barth in the publication of his commentary on *The Epistle to the Romans* had rung loud bells from the belfry. In proclaiming the absolute and unique revelation of the Word of God he had insisted that Christianity should not be called a religion. At the same time Ernst Troeltsch was presenting the view that all religions, including Christianity, are relativized by reason of their historicity. With a narrower perspective psychologists of religion were promoting scientific experiments, for example, to determine the psychophysical effects of organ music and scriptural readings. In other quarters religion was pilloried as the opiate of the masses, the enemy of humanity, and a new day of emancipation from it was being proclaimed with banners and confrontations. In broad circles one could encounter the claim that an old era had come to an end. The dominant philosophies and religious tendencies of the nineteenth century were believed to be at best dead.

The turn in new directions was to be observed in the arts, especially in Expressionism. For a few months I was myself in Germany at about this time, just after Tillich's *The Religious Situation* (1926) had become a best seller. I recall the intense conversations struck up repeatedly, and quite unavoidably, with students in the youth movement whom I encountered at exhibitions of contemporary art. It is not at all surprising that Tillich with his devotion to the plastic arts tells us that in his preparation of his *Philosophy of Religion* he was influenced by contemporary painting, a concern that finds explicit reference in the third essay in the present volume.

Evidence abounds that Tillich was every much "engaged" in the midst of this ferment. In short, the essays of this volume came from the pen of a man who was what Picasso calls "a social creature, always wide-awake in the face of heart-rending bitter or sweet events of the world." In the midst of these events he was aware of both the sense of the irrelevance and the sense of urgency of the question, "What is religion?"

The reference to the Picasso passage cited above possesses still further pertinence for approaching Tillich's philosophy of religion. Tillich was wont to speak of Picasso's *Guernica* as "a great Protestant painting"—not that he found here "the Protestant answer, but rather the radicalism of the Protestant question." This radical quality is especially evident in the closing words of the Picasso passage: "Painting is not made to decorate houses. It is a weapon of offensive and defensive war against the enemy." A basic premise of Tillich's thought is the axiom that authentic religion is not something that can be added as decoration merely to embellish human existence, like a painting "made to decorate houses." It is part and parcel of a struggle.

The essays in the present volume give Tillich's conception of the enemy and also of the power that works against this enemy. False religion represents an important battalion of the enemy, particularly the religion that is only an adjunct of man's existence. The authentic religion is by no means detached from "pulsating life." In Tillich's phrase, it expresses the "pulse beat" of all meaningful existence. But the identification of the enemy is by no means easy. It can be found in what calls itself religion; at the same time the struggle against the enemy can appear in a concealed way where religion appears to be scorned and rejected.

In Tillich's view, then, there is a sense in which religion and even the word "religion" must be rejected as spurious. In considering this meaning of the word he goes so far as to demand the overcoming or "the conquest of the concept of religion."

The essay of this title (1922) has been included in the volume, because it serves as a necessary prologue to his *Philosophy of Religion*. The concept of religion which must be overcome is a concept that in effect destroys the reality to which it is supposed to point. The word "religion" should therefore be taken as a "derogatory term." Tillich gives a number of reasons to justify this pejorative use of the word. For example, what calls itself religion is often simply the appeal to divine sanctions for one or another form of cultural arrogance. This kind of religion "brings no healing." The disastrous consequences are not far to seek. This spurious quality of "religion" is related to another feature, the tendency to interpret religion as simply "a province within the spiritual life." Thus one can hear it said that "just as a person is ethical, scientific, aesthetic or political, so he is at the same time *also* religious."

But in Tillich's view, authentic religion "does not allow a person to be *also* 'religious.'" It does not allow religion to be one concern alongside others. One way in which this spatialization of religion appears is in the effort to assign the religious function to some other function of the human spirit, for example, to the practical (ethical) function, or to feeling, or to intellect (Kant, Schleiermacher [misinterpreted], Hegel). Corresponding to these forms of spatialization is the spatialization of the divine itself: God is understood to be one being alongside other beings, "the Unconditional standing alongside the conditioned."

In all of these ways religion is blunted in its thrust, or it is even perverted; and it cannot be taken with absolute seriousness. Religion and also the object of faith fall into the enclosure and relativity of transient cultural phenomena or of this or that function of the human spirit. God is no longer a consuming fire before these phenomena or functions. Or to use Tillich's fundamental formulation: "The Unconditional is based upon the conditioned, that is, it is destroyed." Men worship a "God under God."

Nevertheless, the concept of religion is unavoidable. It is the purpose of this essay on "the conquest of the concept" to overcome the false concept, that is, to "eliminate" the latter's "destructive force through its subordination to a higher concept, the concept of the Unconditional." In pursuing this purpose Tillich uses the term "religion" to refer to both the authentic and the false, leaving it to the reader to determine by reference to the context which sense of the word is intended.

The reference to the "Unconditional" in this context brings us immediately to one of the characteristic qualities of Tillich's philosophy of religion (as well as of his theology), his desire to avoid traditional language in speaking of religion. Indeed, by reason of his conviction that much of the old language is dead or misleading, he seems to have defined his vocation to be that of framer of a new, or at least of an unfamiliar, language, particularly in order to "overcome" the spurious concepts of religion.

There is an additional characteristically Tillichian feature here in the reference to the "higher concept," the Unconditional. As against a number of the philosophers of idealism Tillich, as we have seen, will not base religion upon any one human function. This would be a false beginning, and would lead to a false concept. Already in a "thesis" he defended in a 1912 academic disputation he had asserted that "the concept of religion must be derived from the concept of God, not the reverse." A philosophy of religion which does not begin with something unconditional never reaches God. In Tillich's philosophy of religion the concept of religion is derived from the concept of the Unconditional. Here Tillich shows himself to represent a special type of philosophy of religion, the type that relies upon intuitional immediacy.

The concept of the Unconditional has "turned off" many a reader. Karl Barth, who for the most part preferred Biblical language, spoke of the term as a "frozen monstrosity." Apparently Tillich chose it not for its positive symbolic power but because it can give rise to freshly minted connotation. The word may be traced at least as far back as Plato, who used it in a different sense; and it bears a one-sided affinity to Anaximander's term "the boundless."

For Tillich the term aims to express the source of the unconditional claim expressed in the demand, "Thou shalt love the Lord thy God with *all* thy heart and with all thy soul, and with all thy mind." It also points beyond the realm of finite differentiations, beyond the cleavage of subject and object, beyond all culture and religion, beyond the human functions; and yet it impinges upon them all. It refers to "a quality but not to a being." In the present volume it is called a symbol for God, though in later writings Tillich speaks of it as "our ultimate, unconditional concern, whether we call it 'God' or 'Being as such' or 'the Good as such' or 'the True as such,' or whether we give it any other name." None of these formulations, however, is entirely adequate, for Tillich's concept of the Unconditional is paradoxical; the Unconditional is related to all finite things, yet it is not one among them or all of them taken together. Moreover, it "stands over against" all things of the finite world (including the concept of God) and at the same time is the dynamic ground of existence and meaning. Besides this, it is the abyss of all meaning, dynamically breaking down encrusted meanings and bursting through to new forms. It is present even in distorted, though partially creative, form in demonic forces, for nothing can exist which is entirely separated from it. Thus the Unconditional in various ways is both affirming and negating. For this reason one may say that it is infinitely apprehensible, yet never entirely comprehensible. Taking all of these ingredients into account, Tillich speaks of the relation between the Unconditional and the conditioned as "the paradoxical immanence of the transcendent." By reason of the paradoxical and dynamic character of the Unconditional Tillich holds that the philosophical method for approaching it is metalogical, a term previously used by Troeltsch.

These ideas are familiar to readers of Tillich, as are a number of the other ideas and terms that appear in his *Philosophy of Religion*. After these necessary preliminary explanations we should turn now to consider the presuppositions and formulations that are to be found in this work as they are presented under the rubric of philosophy of religion.

First let it be said that Tillich in his conception of philosophy of religion has deviated from a generally familiar, conventional conception. According to a conventional conception, philosophy of religion has been defined as a detached systematic study of the concepts or categories of religion toward the end of achieving clarity regarding the character, the structure, and dynamics of the phenomena of religion. Tillich does not adopt this definition. He stems from the tradition of German classical philosophy and also from Existentialism. In this classical tradition philosophy of religion promoted a constructive task, namely, that of presenting a rationale as well as a definition of religion, and of course without ostensible dependence on special revelation. Existentialism for its part has stressed the recognition of the human condition as immediately experienced in its anxiety, its meaninglessness, and its loneliness. With these two outlooks, that of classical German philosophy and that of Existentialism, in his background Tillich sees a more intimate connection between religion and philosophy of religion than has been presupposed in conventional philosophy of religion insofar as it has aimed simply to promote systematic reflection about the phenomenon of religion.

But how is this intimate relation between religion and philosophy of religion to be effected? Viewing the history of the relationship, Tillich recognizes that there has been an antithesis between the two. At certain periods, for example in the early Middle Ages and in the Enlightenment, either theology or philosophy of religion claimed sole sovereignty, in the early Middle Ages the former, in the Enlightenment the latter. In the late Middle Ages, British empiricism, and theological Kantianism, the two disciplines flourished in more or less peaceful coexistence. In the high Middle Ages and in romanticism and philosophical idealism attempts were made in the direction of mediation or of synthesis, in the earlier period from the side of theology and in the later from the side of philosophy. In a special sense Tillich adopts this stance of mediation, asserting that the other types of relationship make for a kind of spiritual schizophrenia.

Tillich approaches the effort to overcome this split (which is only one form of separation in our fragmented world) by defining philosophy of religion as a normative cultural science—what the Germans since Dilthey have called *Geisteswissenschaft*. In his view, philosophy of religion not only studies religion and its categories but it attempts also to achieve a norm regarding authentic religion (here resuming what we have noticed already in the attempt to distinguish authentic from false religion). In contrast to the aim of detached, systematic reflection about religion, Tillich declares that philosophy of religion deals not only with what is but also with what ought to be.

This view of the task of philosophy of religion might seem to be tantamount to equating philosophy of religion and theology. But Tillich rejects this interpretation. In his conception of it philosophy of religion is concerned to delineate the nature of a religion that is valid, yet it relies upon religion or theology to present a concrete articulation of authentic religion. In other words, philosophy of religion is concerned with the criteria of authentic religion but not directly with its realization. In carrying out its task, however, philosophy of religion can make a special contribution by delineating the principal phenomena in terms of basic polarities and alternatives, and also in terms of the relations between religion and culture. Thus philosophy of religion must deal with the categories of religion in both the theoretical and the practical sphere.

But it is not enough to say that philosophy of religion for Tillich is a normative cultural science. Its task is also to overcome the split represented in the antithesis between philosophy of religion and revelational religion. Its aim is to find "the point in the doctrine of revelation and philosophy of religion at which the two are one," and from there "to construct a synthetic solution" of the antithesis. In face of the tension, he says that "the way of synthesis is alone genuine and legitimate."

Tillich repeatedly refers to this synthesis as the goal of his philosophy of religion. It is surprising, however, that this overarching purpose in this work has received extremely little attention. This fact is all the more surprising if we recall that the concept of synthesis was a leitmotiv in the writings of his major predecessors and mentors in philosophy of religion, the German classical philosophers, beginning with Kant and Fichte, and continuing through Hegel, Schelling, Schleiermacher down to Troeltsch. "Synthesis" was the watchword of every philosophy of being and of history devised by the idealists. We should therefore turn our attention to Tillich's conception of synthesis.

* * *

In developing his constructive philosophy of religion Tillich presupposes that an inner unity belongs to all meaningful spiritual life, and that this spiritual life as a whole and in its parts has its root in the divine. The goal of life is the achievement of synthesis, a living unity within a multiplicity. Here Tillich in a general way is in agreement with the idealists. But he cannot accept what he deems to be empty formalism in the Kantian epistemology and ethics, empty primarily because it is cut off from dynamic religious roots. Nor can he accept the optimistic, nontragic synthesis of the Hegelian dialectic or the abstract essentialism of phenomenology, though he appreciates each of these philosophies for certain specified and indispensable contributions to philosophical method. For his part, however, he adopts, or rather adapts, the existential dialectic of Schelling. In doing so, he aims to avoid reductionist intellectualism or rationalism in face of the contradictions of human existence and of reality. He aims also to understand meaninglessness and destructiveness not only as real but also as related to the ground and abyss of the Unconditional. Consequently, he rejects the Hegelian idea of synthesis as sublation, the cancellation and preservation of contrasting elements. The meaningless as complacent or resolute fragmentation, as cynicism, despair, and emptiness, cannot be glossed over. These are the enemy, and they will threaten every meaningful synthesis.

Tillich's philosophy of religion, then, is a philosophy of meaning, and of relatedness to the Unconditional in terms of meaning. The appearance of the concept of meaning immediately suggests the name of Dilthey, for whom it meant the relation of the part to the whole. But Dilthey attempted to interpret meaning without reference to metaphysics. In Tillich's view, the human spirit strives to fulfill the possibilities of being, a meaning-reality that is inescapable and which is never subject to manipulation with impunity. In face of this meaning-reality man's spirit is aware of an interconnection of meaning, indeed of a presence that offers unity of meaning. This unity resides dynamically in the divine ground (and abyss) of meaning, an unconditional meaning. This unconditionality of meaning is alive in every spiritual act, whether theoretical, aesthetic, or practical. It is alive even in doubt. Meaning, then, is threefold. It is an awareness of a universal interconnection of meaning, an awareness of the ultimate meaningfulness of the interconnection of meaning, and an awareness of a demand to fulfill, to be obedient to, the ultimate, unconditional meaning-reality. But the ground of meaning not only makes demand, it is also the source of power that informs every act of meaning, making possible the movement toward fulfillment or synthesis.

Meaning finds expression in forms that have a particular content, but form and content as such do not require more than relatedness to the interconnection of meaning. The second and third elements of meaning just mentioned point to a more foundational element. This element Tillich calls the *import* of meaning, a term (we might add) which Hegel employed in his *Lectures on Aesthetics*. This import of meaning Tillich believed is most readily observable in a painting when it is suffused by a quality that breaks through the form and content.

Authentic religion is directedness toward this import, directedness toward the Unconditional. The awareness of form, content, and import bespeaks a double-directedness of the religious consciousness, that toward the conditioned forms of meaning and their interrelation, and that toward the unconditional meaning-reality which is the ground of the import. Culture is defined as lacking this double-relatedness: it is oriented only to the conditioned forms and the interrelation of meaning. Yet culture is substantially, if not intentionally, religious, for every meaning is supported by the unconditioned meaning-reality.

Now synthesis takes place when the spiritual act is informed by intentional relatedness to this meaning-reality. In cultural creativity, theoretical or practical, synthesis occurs when form and import are conjoined. In this kind of cultural creativity, in this synthesis, the human spirit is engaged in the process of fulfilling being through meaning. Here the interconnection of meaning participates in the depth dimension of the meaning-reality, a ground and an abyss, a support and a negation. This kind of synthesis is an unconditional demand, and if this unity is denied, the path toward meaninglessness is taken.

Synthesis as here understood finds provisional expression in all fully meaningful activity. Tillich's philosophy of religion aims to point to the manifestations of synthesis in all aspects and realms of spiritual life, but also to its frustrations and distortions. Theonomy is the synthesis of autonomy and heteronomy. Authentic religion is the synthesis of its cultural manifestations and relatedness to the Unconditional. Or, in broader terms, "religion and culture come together in their directedness toward the synthesis of forms."

But Tillich's philosophy of religion aims to point not only to the manifestations of synthesis in all aspects and realms of life but also to its frustrations and distortions. The Unconditional is not only support, it is also negation; it is both ground and abyss, grace and judgment. This means that every synthesis must be provisional. Where it is not so considered, we encounter the demonic, a bloated, dynamic self-sufficiency, an aggressive, driving power that is the manifestation of the opposite of grace, "possession." A mortal god is pitted against God.

The whole history of culture and religion can be mapped out in terms of the polarity of the divine and the demonic, of grace and possession. Tillich illustrates the variations on this polarity in an elaborate presentation of the separations and affinities that appear in conceptions of the relations between God and the world, faith and unfaith, religion and culture, the sacred and the secular, autonomy and heteronomy, and even between theocratic (world-shaping) and sacramental motifs. The third essay in the present volume is significant not only because of its striking formulations but also because of its application of his perspectives to the field of the arts as well as to other areas.

In all cases synthesis appears only in the direction toward theonomy, the religion of grace and judgment, the religion of paradox. Since all syntheses are provisional, the absolute synthesis, the universal synthesis, is not something "given." It is a symbol of the plumb line by which all are measured and found wanting; it is the plumb line that symbolizes authentic fulfillment of meaning. Or we may say that it is an eschatological symbol. Yet Tillich believes that it was impressively approached in the high Middle Ages. In principle, if it were generally respected in a society, that society would be moving in the direction of a theonomous cultural synthesis.

* * *

In this fashion Tillich's philosophy of religion aims to fulfill its task of achieving a synthesis between religion and philosophy of religion. In complete separation from each other, or in the attempt to function merely alongside each other, they deny unity, they deny the sovereignty of God over all. The synthesis that he affirms for philosophy of religion is a synthesis he would ask also of theology, the discovery of "the point where the two are one," the point at which both of them share the directedness toward the Unconditional, the point at which both of them are theonomous, and have transcended both autonomy and heteronomy. From this point on theology has its own vocation, to articulate its doctrine of revelation (which belongs to a historical community). We should add here, however, that Tillich the theologian later on changed somewhat his conception of the role of philosophy by assimilating it to his method of correlation wherein it asks questions for theology to answer.

Presumably, philosophy of religion (as presented in this volume) would be able to perform its task of delineating a philosophy of meaning in dialogue with any historical religion. But one must raise the question whether that philosophy of meaning would turn out to be the same as in its present form, for example, if the dialogue were with Buddhism. We raise this question because so many of its present formulations appear to depend upon the Jewish and Christian background, indeed upon a Protestant, and especially Lutheran, background. The religion of paradox set forth appears, for example, to be a restatement of Luther's understanding of God in terms of contrasts as is also the idea about the support and the threat, the Yes and the No, of the Unconditional; the simultaneous Yes and No of grace reflects Luther's doctrine of justification; the contrast between form and import corresponds to that between law and gospel; the fundamentally positive evaluation of the created order wherein "the paradoxical immanence of the transcendence" obtains, presupposes the Biblical doctrine of creation.

To be sure, Tillich in several of his writings has himself insisted that philosophy never exists on a pedestal outside history: it always reflects insights derived ultimately from the confessional religious traditions. For just this reason, one may assume that the philosophy of meaning set forth here would have been different in important ways if the author, even as Westerner and Christian, had taken seriously into account the religious and cultural traditions of the Orient, or if he were a scion of one of these traditions.

Another observation of similar character should be mentioned here. Tillich's philosophy of religion, he would say, stems from the Augustinian-Franciscan tradition wherein the ontological solution of the problem of philosophy of religion obtains. Here, as he has put it, "God is the presupposition of the question of God." This immediate approach is to be contrasted with the mediated approach, the cosmological solution of the problem of philosophy of religion. In the present volume the second approach is not given attention. Thus certain types of problem are evaded. One must look to other writings by Tillich to find them dealt with, though not favorably.

In any event, two things must be said very positively about Tillich's philosophy of religion. First, by his explication of this philosophy of religion he has shown the value, especially for the understanding of the relations between religion and culture, of the concept of meaning. It would be difficult to calculate the number of people (including theological scholars) who under the aegis of the concept of meaning have been led to a new understanding of religion, particularly in its relation to culture. The concept of meaning is here to stay for a long time, even in apologetic literature.

Second, Tillich's elucidation of the different types and dimensions of religion, his description of the dynamics that drive perspectives to their fulfillment or their perversion or their exhaustion, his analysis and criticism of methods for the study of religion, and also his exemplification of a constructive philosophy of religion, exhibit rare skill and insight. For the careful reader they offer substantial assistance to become "wide-awake in the face of heart-rending bitter or sweet events of the world" of religion and culture.

The first two essays translated here are to be found in Paul Tillich, *Gesammelte Werke,* I, the third essay, in GW IX (Stuttgart: Evangelisches Verlagswerk). The editor wishes to express here warm gratitude to Professor Charles W. Fox for substantial assistance in the translation of these essays, particularly in the effort to achieve consistency in the rendering of technical terms.

What Is Religion?

I
The Philosophy of Religion*

INTRODUCTION §
SUBJECT MATTER AND METHOD OF
PHILOSOPHY OF RELIGION

———— §§§ ————

a. Religion and Philosophy of Religion

The subject matter of philosophy of religion is religion. This elementary definition, however, raises a problem at the outset. It is, generally speaking, the basic problem of the philosophy of religion. In religion, philosophy encounters something that resists becoming an object of philosophy. The stronger, purer, and more original the religion, the more emphatically it makes the claim to be exempt from all generalizing conceptual structures. Concepts such as "revelation" and "redemption" stand in clear opposition to the concept of "religion." They express an action happening only once, transcendent in origin and transforming in its effect on re-

---

* Translated by James Luther Adams, Konrad Raiser and Charles W. Fox.

27

ality, while "religion" subordinates a whole series of spirtual acts and cultural creations under a general concept. "Revelation" speaks of a divine, "religion" of a human, action. "Revelation" speaks of an absolute, singular, exclusive, and self-sufficient happening; "religion" refers to merely relative occurrences, always recurring and never exclusive. "Revelation" speaks of the entrance of a new reality into life and the spirit; "religion" speaks of a given reality of life and a necessary function of the spirit. "Religion" speaks of culture, "revelation" of that which lies beyond culture. For this reason religion feels an assault is made upon its inmost essence when it is called religion. For that reason it closes its mind to philosophy of religion and opens itself at most to theology, insofar as the latter is nothing other than a "science" of revelation. Thus philosophy of religion is in a peculiar position in face of religion. It must either dissolve away the object it wishes to grasp or declare itself null and void. If it does not recognize religion's claim to revelation, then it misses its object and does not speak of genuine religion. If, on the other hand, it acknowledges the claim to revelation, then it becomes theology.

Philosophy of religion can travel neither of these paths. The first leads it astray from its goal. The second leads to the dissolution not only of philosophy of religion but also of philosophy generally. If there is one object that remains fundamentally closed to philosophy, then philosophy's claim over every object is brought into question. For then it would certainly be in no position to draw for itself the borderline between this reserved subject matter (i.e., religion) and other fields of research. In fact, it might be possible that revelation would extend its claim to all disciplines, and that philosophy would have no weapon with which to resist this claim. If it surrenders at one point, it must surrender at every point. As a matter of fact, revelation does make this claim.

If revelation is the breakthrough of the Unconditional into the world of the conditioned, it cannot let itself be made into something conditioned, becoming one sphere alongside others, religion alongside culture. It must rather consider the truth it proclaims as the foundation of all knowledge of truth. It must set up a theology of knowledge in place of a philosophy of religion, and it must add to this a theology of art, of law, of community, etc. It cannot admit that there is a conditioned perspective of equal value alongside its unconditioned perspective. To do that would be to annul its own unconditionality.

This antithesis between philosophy of religion and the doctrine of revelation poses the problem of philosophy of religion in its most acute form. It is not only a dialectical problem. The reality of the problem becomes evident when we consider the fact that it has led to both the most serious conflicts and the most powerful creations of culture. In its entire range the cultural history of philosophy and religion reveals phenomena in which one or the other of these forms attains almost pure realization. The early Middle Ages could serve as an example for the one approach, and the Enlightenment for the other. On the other hand, we discover attempts at mediation between or at synthesis of the two positions, as is true for the high Middle Ages from the side of the doctrine of revelation, and for idealism and romanticism from the side of philosophy. Finally, there are periods in which the two are maintained alongside each other, as in the late Middle Ages, British empiricism and theological Kantianism. But no marking off of boundaries can bring about a solution. It denies the philosophical conviction of truth as much as it denies the unconditionality of revelation to allow either of them to be forced into one sphere alongside others. Every attempt of this kind must miscarry. As a way of answering the question who should determine the limits of the two disciplines, the method of demarcating boundaries fails by necessity, because both sides claim this right. And yet the opposition cannot be allowed to remain, for it leads to the shattering of the unity of consciousness and to the dissolution of religion or culture. As long as a naïve faith holds one position or the other as obviously authoritative—whether it be the doctrine of revelation or philosophy—and derogates the other position as subsidiary, the conflict is disguised. But once the naïveté is shattered—the philosophical as well as the religious—only the synthetic solution remains. Every other escape is cut off. A calculated return to naïveté is a delusive step. Only the way forward remains, namely, the way toward the inner overcoming of the antithesis. The way of synthesis alone is genuine and legitimate. It is required, even if it fails again and again. But it is not necessary that it fail. For there is a point in the doctrine of revelation and philosophy at which the two are one. To find this point and from there to construct a synthetic solution is the decisive task of the philosophy of religion.

b. The Place of Philosophy of Religion in the System of Knowledge.[1]

The demand must be made of every systematic presentation of an individual discipline that it define its place in *the system of the sciences* (or of knowledge) as to subject matter and method. This is especially true for the normative cultural sciences (*Geisteswissenschaften*), in which subject matter and method belong more closely together, and in which they are to a much higher degree disputable, than in the purely formal and empirical sciences (*Denk- und Seinswissenschaften*). It is true above all for philosophy of

---

[1] Regarding this and the following sections see my *System der Wissenschaften* (Göttingen, 1923), reprinted in *Gesammelte Werke*, Vol. I (Stuttgart, 1959).

religion, whose initial problem is its right of individual existence among the other sciences. Incorrect determinations of the relation of philosophy of religion to the other disciplines make the solution of the basic problem of philosophy of religion impossible from the outset. Philosophy of religion is from the beginning dependent upon the systematic theory of knowledge (*Wissenschaftssyste-matik*). But the dependence is mutual. The system of the sciences is conditioned by the conception of the individual disciplines, and since science in general is brought into question by the basic problem of philosophy of religion, it is conditioned especially by philosophy of religion. The systematic theory of the sciences is in its totality dependent upon the solution of the problem of philosophy of religion. This reciprocity corresponds to the living character of knowledge. It signifies that all aspects of knowing are conditioned by the basic, systematic insight into the nature of things (*Wesens-schau*). This does not exclude the individual elements, however, from being considered successively in their own right, and then being incorporated into a onesided fundamental framework. Therefore, we begin with a discussion of the system of knowledge. But we are aware that this is contingent upon the solution of the basic problem of the philosophy of religion. There are three questions we wish to answer: (1) the relation of philosophy of religion to the empirical science of religion; (2) the place of philosophy of religion in the system of the normative cultural sciences, particularly its relation to philosophy in general and to theology; and (3) the relation of philosophy of religion to metaphysics.

Philosophy of religion belongs to the cultural or normative sciences. It sets forth in a creative and productive synthesis what is valid as religion. It employs for its normative construction the materials provided by the history of religions, the psychology of religion, and the sociology of religion. But it is not identical, either entirely or in part, with any of these empirical disciplines. Its task is not to consider what actually is (*Seiendes*) but rather what ought to be (*Gültiges*). Factual data serve as material to be used in its constructive work, but they are not the goal of its work. The methodology of the cultural sciences determines the manner in which this empirical material will function. Thus the attempt to assign to philosophy of religion, directly or indirectly, tasks that should be accomplished by history and by the psychology and sociology of culture, must be repudiated. This includes every kind of theory of types, for the concept of type represents the aim of the study of forms, especially in psychology and sociology—but it does not represent a goal of knowledge for the cultural or normative sciences.

Any presentation of the cultural sciences contains three elements: a philosophy, a cultural history, and a systematics (*Systematik*). In philosophy the particular sphere of meaning and its categories are articulated. In cultural history the material that the empirical sciences present is systematically understood and arranged. In systematics the concrete normative system is presented on the basis of the philosophical conception of the essence of the particular matter in hand and on the basis of the historical material understood in the light of cultural-historical construction. Every genuine cultural science consciously or unconsciously proceeds in this threefold way. It proceeds from a universal function of the spirit and the forms through which objects are constituted therein. It then shows in a critical way the actualization of this essential function in the various directions of historical development. Finally, it gives its own systematic solution on the basis of the problems that are brought to the fore by the conceptualization of the essence of the thing and by the cultural history. This threefold relationship appears as the philosophy of art, the cultural history of art, and normative aesthetics; or as the philosophy of knowing (*Erkennen*), the cultural history of science, and a normative theory of science; or as the philosophy of law, the cultural history of law, and a normative theory of law, etc. The same threefold relationship is evident in philosophy of religion, the cultural history of religion, and the systematic theory of religion or theology.

With this in mind we can state provisionally the task of philosophy of religion and its relation to theology. Philosophy of religion is the theory of the religious function and its categories. Theology is the normative and systematic presentation of the concrete realization of the concept of "religion." The cultural history of religion acts as a bridge between philosophy of religion and theology. It grasps critically the individual realizations of the concept of religion in history and thereby leads on to a special systematic solution of its own (which can be the solution of a group, a "school," or a church). Thus philosophy of religion and theology are two elements of a single normative cultural science of religion. They belong inseparably together and are in continual interaction with each other and with the third element, the cultural history of religion. For this reason no one of the three elements should without hesitation be given special emphasis in the presentation of a normative science. The separation of philosophy of religion and theology is no better founded than the separation of philosophy of art and normative aesthetics, or of moral philosophy and normative ethics. These separations are justified only for the sake of a division of labor, but not in terms of the subject matter. And wherever these separations are made, the mutual dependence of the elements persists, even if it is not recognized. Every theology is dependent upon the presupposition of a concept of the essence of religion. Every philosophy of religion is depen-

dent upon a concept of the norm of religion. And both are dependent upon comprehension of the cultural-historical material. On
this basis we shall consider in detail the philosophy of religion
proper, that is, the theory of the essence and categories of the
religious sphere. On the other hand, we shall consider the cultural
history of religion briefly to indicate its main tendencies, and theology solely in connection with the general definition of the concept
of the norm of religion. Philosophy of religion would remain
abstract and indistinct if cultural history and theology were not
also taken into account. On the other hand, a complete presentation of both the other elements would lead out of the particular
frame of reference of philosophy of religion and into a system of
the normative science of religion in general. Such a procedure
would in fact be the scientific ideal.

The definitions given above for the relationship of philosophy
of religion and theology have passed over the basic problem of
philosophy of religion. They have treated religion as one function
alongside others, and theology as one discipline alongside others.
It is now necessary to discuss the relation of religion to the other
spheres of meaning and accordingly to examine the relation of the
normative science of religion to the other cultural sciences. This is
possible, however, only through the definition of the essence of
religion, that is, by anticipating what is to be set forth in what follows. Only this much can be said: The "alongsidedness" must not
be permitted to stand; that is, religion and theology must not remain
alongside the other functions and sciences. The synthesis under discussion in the first section of this essay can be attained only if the
normative science of religion is in some sense a normative cultural
science in general, and only if religion is presented not as one
function alongside others but as an attitude in all the other functions. The concept of religion must itself show in what sense that
is the case.

The task now still remains to clarify the relation of philosophy of religion to metaphysics. All controversies about metaphysics are fruitless insofar as one does not recognize that it is not a science but an independent function of the mind, and that it is accordingly not a problem within the sciences as to how they are related to each other, but a problem of the philosophy of spirit as such (*Geistesphilosophie überhaupt*). All the errors of metaphysics spring from the attempt to make it a science alongside or above the other sciences. It is insight into the independence of the metaphysical attitude which alone makes possible a conception that gives a rightful place to both science and metaphysics. To be sure, even at this point the difficulty arises that a complete clarification of the essence of metaphysics is not possible without philosophy of religion. For metaphysics is necessarily and at all times a religious attitude. It is directedness toward the Unconditional (*Richtung auf das Unbedingte*) in the theoretical sphere of the functions of the spirit. Only so long as it is thus conceived, that is, only so long as it is religious, does it have independent existence. And only thus is it kept from falling into the status of a sham science. It follows from this that a philosophy of metaphysics, that is, a theory of the essence and categories of the metaphysical function, is impossible without a philosophy of religion. In order that philosophy of religion may be free from metaphysical taints, the following definition of the relation between science and metaphysics may be given. Metaphysics, together with the scientific and the aesthetic functions, forms the group of theoretical and world-embracing functions of meaning. To be sure, metaphysics stands over against both of these insofar as it unites in itself a scientific and an aesthetic element, and is not like them directed to conditioned forms but toward the Unconditional itself. But since human consciousness has no other forms than those which are conditioned, it must use these in order to express the Unconditional in them. This means that it must use scientific concepts symbolically and not literally. Science provides the symbols for metaphysics, but these symbols are selected not in terms of their validity (*Geltungswert*), that is, not scientifically, but for their expressive values (*Ausdruckswert*), that is, aesthetically. Conversely, in every act of apprehending the conditioned forms the ultimate attitude or relation to the Unconditional is a decisive element, whether it involve aesthetic style or scientific method. The metaphysical attitude (not the system of metaphysical symbols) is determinative for both. Metaphysics functions not as a science, but as a spiritual attitude influencing science. This is the interdependence that at the same time permits a complete mutual freedom and makes it possible for philosophy of religion to begin its work without reference to a metaphysical symbolism.

From this special relationship between science and metaphysics is to be distinguished the general relationship that obtains between science and every function of meaning, insofar as science wishes to grasp the latter scientifically. Here the way in which knowledge functions in relation to metaphysics is in no way different from its functioning in relation to art, law, science, ethos, etc. In relation to the functions of meaning, the knowing process is always receptive as well as productive. It is determined by the independent, creative process of every sphere of meaning. It is, however, at the same time determinative for that process. The act of knowing in the cultural sciences stands over against its object not merely objectively, but in the process of knowing the object it is itself affected. The act of knowing in the cultural sciences is a systematic bringing to consciousness of the creative spiritual process, and as such is simultaneously determinative for the process itself. Thus the theory of science or knowledge (*Wissenschaftslehre*) affects the scientific process, the theory of art affects the creation of art, the theory of law affects the legislative process, and in the same way the theory of metaphysics affects the metaphysical stance. But just as the theory of art does not produce the art process, but merely co-determines it, so the theory of metaphysics does not produce metaphysics, but it affects its conscious formation.

Thus the question of the relation between philosophy of religion and metaphysics gains decisive importance through the question concerning the relation between religion and metaphysics. But the answer to this question belongs in philosophy of religion itself, and cannot be settled as a preliminary question.

c. The Method of Philosophy of Religion

(i) METHODS ALIEN TO PHILOSOPHY OF RELIGION

The method of philosophy of religion is identical with the method of normative *Geisteswissenschaft* in general. But since no agreement obtains concerning this method, and since as a consequence of the individual, creative character of the cultural sciences such agreement can obtain only in a very limited way, it is necessary that every cultural-scientific investigation make clear its methodological principles. This is especially true for philosophy of religion, for alongside the general methodological problems of cultural science special problems must be taken into account which proceed from the individual character of its subject matter. All methods in philosophy of religion which come to it from the science of religion or from theology and metaphysics, are heterogeneous. The empirical, the supernatural, and the speculative methods are of this character.

The method of the empirical sciences is heterogeneous to that of philosophy of religion. The latter does not make religion an object of psychological, sociological, and historical consideration. It is based neither on psychology of religion nor on sociology of religion, nor on history of religion. It proceeds from the knowledge that a concept of essence in the realm of spirit is to be grasped neither through abstraction from individual phenomena nor through the consideration of its origin and formation in a particular object in society or in the whole of history.

Abstraction presupposes an awareness of that which is to be acquired through abstraction. For without such an awareness the range of phenomena on the basis of which abstraction is to take place would be vague and arbitrary. In order to decide whether Buddhism or the like comes into consideration for the definition of the essence of religion one must previously decide what is meant by religion. Accordingly, that decision can not be made by abstraction from these phenomena. The same holds also for the psychological, sociological, and evolutionary explanations of religion. Either they must presuppose in advance what religion is, and they can then indicate the forms in which religion appears in individual and social life; but they cannot in this way determine the essence of religion in itself. Or if they want to determine the essence of religion itself by such explanations, they must assume that religion does not have one single essence, but is a collection of extra-religious elements. This means that the genetic method presupposes a negative a priori concept of essence if it wishes to be philosophy of religion, while the method of abstraction presupposes a positive a priori concept. But whether an essence of religion be recognized or not, whether the a priori be positive or negative, it is not in any case acquired from experience but is brought to experience, and is determinative for the direction of the whole process.

The method of psychological understanding (*verstehende Psychologie*) tries to do justice to this state of affairs. According to this method, the religious life is to be understood on the basis of one's own religious experience, and this individual experience in turn may be clarified and purified through the understanding of the religious lives of others. In this psychological "circle," in this "to and fro" of one's own experience and understanding the experience of others, knowledge of the essence of religion is to develop. The introduction of this circular principle as a methodological axiom no doubt has put an end to the self-deceptions of the empirical methods that claim to be objective. But the fundamental defect of empirical method in general is not overcome by the circular principle. Religious experience, on the basis of which the religious life should be understood, is itself an indefinite and, from the point of view of method, accidental datum. Moreover, one cannot see why religious experience is supposed to acquire objective validity by understanding the religious experience of others and by being shaped by it, for this is likewise accidental and undefined. The reciprocal action of two or even of many actualities cannot itself produce anything valid. The psychological method of the "psychological circle" only has claim if it presupposes that a valid, transcendent form is involved in one's own experience and in empathy with the experience of others. But it then ceases to be the psychological method, and becomes the critical and phenomenological method.

Back of the method of the psychological circle stands historically and logically the theological method. This is the attempt to derive the concept of religion from one's own revealed, and therefore true, religion. The difference is only that the psychological method has given up the supernatural presupposition of the miraculous character of one's own experience, and therefore can freely acknowledge the other religions. The point of departure, however, remains the same, that is, one's own religion. The specifically theological method proceeds from a concept of the norm of religion, and derives from it the concept of the essence of religion. It is empirical, even though it limits its empiricism to *one* super-naturally designated place. It depends on the opposition of true and false religion, but it is not consistent in doing so. If it were, it would not permit a concept of the essence of religion to be sought at all. It would have to repudiate the concept of religion as an attempt to place the true and the false on the same level. It would not be at liberty to make the claim to be philosophy of religion, and would have to remain theology, a normative theory of religion.

In contrast to the empirical methods stands the speculative method. While the former methods attempt to proceed from the religious function and to deduce the essence of religion from the religious act, the speculative method tries to determine the essence of religion from the object toward which the act itself is directed. The way to the knowledge of the essence of religion is accordingly thought to be identical with the way of knowing the religious object, that is, with metaphysics. If the religious object is determined metaphysically, then religion is defined as the sum total of the theoretical and practical acts directed toward the object. But this method also contains an inner contradiction. It assumes that the religious object can be grasped apart from religious acts. It assumes that the Unconditional is an object of rational knowledge, that metaphysics is a science. But this supposition is false. The Unconditional is not given otherwise than in religious acts, and metaphysics is the religious act in which the Unconditional is grasped in theoretical and rational symbols. It is for that reason impossible to grasp the religious object apart from the religious act. This is the core of all criticism of the speculative method.

Consideration of the methods mentioned so far has led to negative results. They do not attain the vantage of the cultural sciences. And yet they are not of merely negative value. They set up demands for the completely satisfactory method. The method of the history of religion demands from the concept of the essence of religion that it make intelligible every possible religious phenomenon. The method of psychological understanding (*verstehende Psychologie*) recognizes that spiritual realities must be immediately given to the subject. The theological method demands an unequivocally valid concept of the nature of religion which is independent of subjective psychological contingency. Finally, the speculative method demands that the religious object as well as the religious act be taken into account in the concept of the essence of religion. These demands must be fulfilled by the method proper to the philosophy of religion.

(ii) METHODS PROPER TO THE PHILOSOPHY OF RELIGION

Philosophy is the science of the functions of meaning and their categories. It is the first, basic element of every normative cultural science. Upon it the cultural history and also the systematic theory of norms are constructed. Thus philosophy of religion is the science of the religious function of meaning and its categories. A function of meaning is comprehended when one shows the necessary place it occupies in the structure of meaning-reality (*Sinnwirklichkeit*). Consequently, a dual demand is placed upon philosophical method. It must abstract the formative principles from the reality that is informed by meaning. And it must bring the principles of meaning into a unified and necessary relationship. Insofar as philosophy abstracts the principles of meaning from the meaning-reality, it is *critical*. Insofar as it systematically relates the principles of meaning to each other, it is *dialectical*. Both methods, however, are one: the critical method is always dialectical as well. For there is no possibility of articulating the principles of meaning from the meaning-reality other than by demonstrating their necessity for the construction of a unified order of being (*Seinswelt*); and the dialectical method is necessarily also critical, for a necessary interconnection of meaning (*Sinnzusammenhang*) appears only in a system of the principles of meaning and not in the meaning-reality itself. Where the critical method neglects the dialectical element, it will not be free from empirically accidental concepts in the delineation of the functions and the categories (as, for example, in Kant). Where the dialectical method forgets the critical element, it becomes an inadmissible metaphysic of being and history (as, for example, in Hegel).

The critical-dialectical method presupposes the autonomy of the spiritual over against every immediately given existing thing (*unmittelbar Seiendes*). But it does not need on that account to advocate an epistemological idealism. It need not assume that spirit gives laws to nature. Nevertheless, it cannot hold an epistemological realism to be true. It cannot assume that nature gives laws to the spirit. It must assume that the principles of meaning to which consciousness submits itself in the spiritual act are at the same time the principles of meaning to which being is subjected. It must assume that the meaning of being comes to expression in the consciousness informed by meaning. If it hopes in this matter to avoid the difficulties of an exclusive idealism as well as of a doctrine of pre-established harmony, then it is best to speak of the spiritual process fulfilling being through meaning (*Sinnerfüllung des Seins*). On this premise, which is ultimately nothing other than a self-apprehension of the spirit as spirit and not as being, the critical-dialectical method develops the universal forms of meaning, which are at the same time functions of the spirit and principles of the meaning-reality.

Although critical-dialectical activity is the basic element of every cultural-scientific and philosophical method, it is nevertheless not its only element. The critical method, especially in the development it has undergone in Kant and in the Neo-Kantian school, investigates the preconditions of a unified structure in the meaning-reality. It is directed toward the interconnection of the forms of meaning. It separates the principles of meaning from all the contents of the meaning-reality, and subordinates them to the fundamental logical principle of unity. By this means, however, it involves only the one element inherent in all consciousness of meaning, namely, the *form* of meaning, while it misses the *import* or *substance* of meaning. The import of meaning is the ground of reality presupposed in all forms of meaning, upon whose constant presence the ultimate meaningfulness, the significance, and the essentiality (*Wesenhaftigkeit*) of every act of meaning rest. The unity of forms, like every individual form, is utterly empty without the relation to the import of meaning. Now the critical method, insofar as it presents the unity of the forms of meaning, may abstract from this import; it can trace out the purely logical-dialectical relations of the separate principles, and it then finds itself in possession of a system of forms—which, to be sure, are absolutely empty. The reproach of emptiness or formalism against a system of scientific concepts would be completely unjustified if these concepts were appropriate to the objects they are supposed to grasp. This, however, is not the case. In the pure critical method all the principles of meaning appear in logistic abridgement. They are seen only so far as they have a purely logically apprehensible dimension related to a formal unity. The dimension related to import and the metalogical forms resulting from the dialectic of form and import are not grasped by this means.

This holds for all theoretical and practical functions. But it holds basically for philosophy of religion. Wherever the critical philosophy of religion is carried through without metaphysical admixtures, it arrives at the conception of religion as orientation to the unity of the forms of meaning, to the absolute synthesis of the functions. There are all kinds of attempts to merge religion with one of the other functions or to make it a special function beside the others. But these attempts fail by reason of the impossibility of establishing a dialectical basis for such a function in the system of the forms of meaning. No place is found for this function; and thus it is identified with the unity of forms. This is undoubtedly justified in the critical system, and it is also grounded in the subject matter itself. But it is not satisfactory. At this point the basic problem of philosophy of religion becomes immediately significant for the delineation of the method itself. Religion objects to being turned into a synthesis of the spiritual functions. It gives expression to this by refusing to admit a parity between the divine and the human, the holy and the natural spirit. It points to the radical difference between the Holy and every cultural phenomenon. If this sheer opposition is taken over into the philosophy of religion, it can lead to a complete repudiation of the critical method. This would undoubtedly be justified if the critical element had to be the only element of the philosophical method. As a matter of fact, a method that cannot grasp concepts such as grace, revelation and the demonic, which break through all forms, is absolutely inadequate for religion. The critical element, however, must not remain the only element.

The most vigorous criticism of the critical method today comes from phenomenology. This is the attempt to construct a system of essences through the recovery of logical realism—a system that is brought to consciousness by an immediate intuition of essences (*Wesensschau*). Every essence is a priori. Empiricism furnishes only the material of intuition in which the essence is perceived. However, the essence itself is not empirical. The rational, formal character of the critical a priori is thereby overcome. The phenomenological a priori is the vivid, intuited essence itself. The distinction between the formal principles of meaning and the contents that are determined empirically is done away with so far as the sphere of essences is concerned. As a result, the intuition of essences extends uniformly to all objects, spiritual and sentient. In place of distinguishing between being and spirit, phenomenology distinguishes between essence and existence. Essence is the fullness or completeness in which existing things more or less participate. It is the eternal truth of existing things. The intuition of essence can be occasioned by any object, real or imaginary. It is true when it penetrates to the essence. According to the phenomenological method, a philosophy of religion would therefore be able to intuit the essence and the peculiar qualities of religion in any example of it. It would be independent of the empirical and yet would have an a priori rich in content and not merely formal. It is consequently supposed to have no difficulty in recognizing the uniqueness of religion over against all other spiritual essences, for it has no other task than to intuit essences. Existential problems emerge beyond its borders. If one had to choose between the critical and the phenomenological method, phenomenology without any doubt would be preferable for philosophy of religion. It is able to approach the real object of inquiry more closely and vitally than is possible for either criticism or dialectic. It lives in the very thing itself, not in its rational-abstract aspect.

Weighty objections, however, in both methodology and principle, qualify this merit of phenomenology. These objections are based on the relationship that obtains between essence and existence. For phenomenological realism, existence originates only in an accidental and ultimately indifferent coming together of distinct essential attributes in one individual. The individual has no advantage beyond sheer existence, over the essential attributes in which it participates. The inner infinity and eternal significance of the individual are blotted out. This consequence is especially disastrous for history. For phenomenology has no organ for apprehending the uniquely creative character of the historical event. Thus, as for example in philosophy of religion, it would have to establish an "essence" of religion that transcends all empirical religion and yet that possesses content. This essence either bears the features of one particular religion, as is evident in the actual application of the method, or it constructs a new, ideal religion. In the first case a methodologically inadmissible traditionalism emerges which comes very near to the supernatural method. In the second case a constructive rationalism could be avoided only if a prophetically religious view rather than a methodological science were involved. It will not do, however, to equate the concept of essence and the concept of norm. Only if the concept of essence retains a formal character does it leave room for a material fulfillment through history and for a concept of norm which is consciously created from history and which justifiably displays the features of a historical sequence of tradition.

Phenomenology faces this alternative: Either it can interpret the individual historical reality as an insignificant manifestation of essence, in order to be able to undertake the intuiting of essence in any and every religious phenomenon; or it can offer a proof (a procedure that could not be phenomenological) as to why just one particular phenomenon is employed as the material for the intuition of essence. Phenomenology is right in cases where the essence is related to the phenomenon as the mathematical triangle is to an actual one, that is, where the phenomenon is nothing more than concrete illustration. This means, however, that with respect to history phenomenology is wrong.

Criticism of the phenomenological method on the basis of the individual-creative character of historical phenomena forces us to define our position over against the method that affirms the individual by rejecting the universal. We refer to the version of nominalism which today has become significant in the form of pragmatism and the "Philosophy of 'As If.'" It regards concepts as subjective constructions, as words or fictions, which have meaning for life but no reality in the sense of objective truth. Their meaning for life consists in the fact that they facilitate the control exercised by an organism or a species of being, especially of mankind, over the environment and the inner world, thus strengthening the power of life in the subject that devises the concepts. To understand a reality like religion means therefore to indicate the life-enhancing significance of the religious fiction, to point out the place in the life-process at which this fiction necessarily arises. The pragmatic method takes the individual-creative character of the living reality into fullest account. It is in the sharpest opposition to every rational, intuitive, or supernatural fixation of spiritual essences. But it is subject to the fundamental objection that it is by nature life-destroying, and can therefore be tolerated only by a spiritual attitude for which theory remains theory and does not become living conviction. Moreover, it contains in itself the ineradicable antithesis that at the moment when by its victory it destroys life, the only criterion for the truth of a fiction which it accepts, namely, its life-strengthening power, turns against itself. For that reason the pragmatic method must be rejected for philosophy of religion.

The critical, phenomenological and pragmatic methods are determined on the one hand by logical considerations. On the other they are, like every basic methodological attitude, the expression of a general spiritual situation (*Geisteslage*). A discussion of these methods must not fail to show this ultimate metaphysical back-

47

ground by means of which alone their spiritual import can really be understood. The phenomenological method is the expression of an attitude that turns away from the world of appearance to the inner essence of things. This inversion of the natural view of the world, this inner intuition of essences, contains a mystical and ascetic element and is the expression of a static metaphysics and of the desire to achieve union with the eternally abiding reality through an act of knowledge. The equating of the concept of essence with the concept of norm presupposes a spiritual situation in which a self-sufficient world view shut off from criticism is dominant, and for that reason the given spiritual forms of life can become immediate examples of eternal essences. In the field of epistemology the phenomenological method is the authentic expression for such a spiritual situation. As soon, however, as the unity and the immediate certainty of the traditional meaning-reality is broken by the fateful course of history, and as soon as concern for changing appearances has replaced preoccupation with eternal essences, then phenomenology loses its deepest meaning. It cannot do justice to the problem of existence, and retains only the significance of a standing protest against the exclusively critical and formal attitude.

In full opposition to phenomenology the pragmatic method in general refuses to recognize anything static in things or anything connected with the idea of essence. It considers a concept to be an act of object-manipulation which can be changed at every instant and which is a transitional moment in the dynamics of power relations; and this concept is the only thing that can be affirmed as an "essence" of the world. Standing behind this method is the spirit of an active technological, world-transforming attitude, oriented to Becoming. It presupposes the dissolution of all comprehensive spiritual unities. It knows only the concept of norm and not the concept of essence. As a consequence of this, the concept of norm changes together with the subject that posits the norm, without claiming to have anything to do with essence. The pragmatic method is the epistemologically formulated renunciation of knowledge. The significance that it nevertheless has for knowing is its insight into the individual-creative character of all normative concepts in the realm of spirit, and its awareness of the dynamic, creative character of existence, a creativity that transforms even essences.

Between the phenomenological and the pragmatic spiritual situation stands the situation determined by the critical-dialectical attitude. It no longer possesses the unity inherent in an immediately given order of convictions. But it is not ready to throw itself unreservedly into the stream of dynamic subjectivism. It believes in a transcending spirit, in validity of meaning, but it cannot intuit and grasp it in terms of its content, and therefore constructs it critically out of the form. But the form is empty, and where it dominates it empties the living content and replaces it with a rational scheme the filling out of which is supposed to be provided by an endlessly advancing empiricism. This method is the expression of a critical detachment from an immediately given, unified and self-sufficient order of convictions. It is the attitude of protest not for the sake of caprice but for the sake of the pure form. It is a heroic attitude that would rather dwell in the emptiness of pure form than in the mystical fullness of static essences that no longer carry with them the power of conviction, or in the biological fullness of dynamic laws of nature which are bound to no form. It is a turning back to existence, to the empirical order and history, but not a direct return; it is rather a return that has been conditioned by rational form. Heroism and criticism, however, are only forms of transition or change and not forms of life. They live either from the old contents that they dissolve through criticism or from the new ideal that they construct through reason. But they do not live from a power of their own. And for that reason the critical method, just as surely as it gives expression to the unique fate of the Western world, is a transitional method. The continuation and transformation of this method is the cultural-historical demand of our day. If this demand is not met, then the cleavage of our spiritual life into a romantically conceived mysticism of essence and an arbitrary dynamism that goes beyond the very realm of spirit is unavoidable. The fate of the cultural sciences and the possibility of a solution of the basic problems of philosophy of religion depend upon the extension of the critical method in response to the demands of phenomenology and pragmatism. For whereas pure pragmatism leads out of the sphere of science or knowledge altogether, pure phenomenology is an explication of the concept of the religious norm, and thus it is theology and not philosophy of religion; and pure criticism is a philosophy that does not perceive the negative character of the religious sphere in face of philosophy of religion, and for this reason dissolves away religion, the very thing it seeks to understand.

(iii) THE METALOGICAL METHOD

When the critical method is modified in terms of the intuitional and the dynamic methods we call it *metalogical*. It is *logical* in the sense that the orientation to pure rational forms, involved in the critical method, is retained. It is *meta*logical because it goes beyond pure formalism in a double sense, on the one hand in that it apprehends the import inhering in the forms, on the other in that it sets up norms in an individual-creative way. The metalogical method is based on the critico-dialectical method. Like the latter, it abstracts the functions and categories of meaning from the meaning-reality, and brings them as the conditioning factors of a meaningful construction of reality into a necessary dialectical connection. A function and a category are recognized in terms of both their essence and their necessity when their place in the construction of the meaning-reality is discovered.

The critical element, however, is not the only element of the metalogical method. That aspect of functions and categories which is related to import should also be taken into account. The living dialectic of the elements of meaning (*i.e.,* of form and import) which penetrates the whole of reality, should be grasped. Metalogical intuition of essences is not directed toward particular things and qualities: it does not remain attached to the individual form, but rather it perceives the tensions and polarities that seem to it to constitute the really essential element in the essence. The intuition (*Schau*) of the inner *dynamic* in the structure of the meaning-reality is the goal of metalogic. In this process, it draws a sharp line between the forms of meaning and the objects of meaning. It is directed only toward the forms of meaning, the functions and categories through which the objects or realizations of meaning are constituted, but which are not themselves objects. On the other hand, it leaves the objects of meaning, the living wholes (*Gestalten*) of nature and history, to empirical investigations supported by the categorial intuition of essences. Just because it knows of the infinite tension between form and import it cannot even consider trying to apprehend the objects of meaning metalogically in the manner of the Hegelian dialectic or of Schelling's system of nature. The awareness of the infinity of everything real makes such an intention impossible.

Contrasted with phenomenology, the peculiarity of metalogic can therefore be defined in two ways. On the one hand metalogic does not remain attached to particular forms, but rather reaches back critically and intuitively to the principles of meaning which are conditioned by both form and import, upon the apprehension of which all particular intuitions of essence depend. On the other hand, it cedes the apprehension of particulars to empiricism—of course not to every kind of empiricism, but rather to an empiricism guided and supported by the categorial apprehension of essences. It therefore parcels out the phenomenological realm of essences, on the one hand to the dynamic dialectic of the elements of meaning, and on the other to objective experience. It thus achieves on the one hand a basis for criticism (which is lacking in phenomenology) without becoming formalistic, and on the other it raises empiricism to the height of a living intuition of essences, without thereby having to posit, like phenomenology, a second mystical empiricism beside the objective one.

Nevertheless, the way of metalogic is not without some relation to mysticism, namely, to its intuitive element. The basic insight of all mysticism, that the principles of the macrocosm are given in the microcosm, finds its epistemological expression in the theory of the spirit fulfilling being through meaning. This signifies, however, that the elements of every meaning, form and import, are the essential elements of everything as such. The apprehension of the import of meaning has used symbols, especially in Occidental mysticism, which are derived from psychological language: the ground of the soul, the unconscious, the will, and the like. The last-named concept has gained great significance through the voluntaristic metaphysics of Boehme, Baader, Schelling, Schopenhauer, Nietzsche, and others. In this process the symbolic character of the concept of the will has often been misunderstood and the great mystical epistemological conception of it thus has been forced down to the level of a rational, and hence impossible, biological or psychological metaphysics. It has not been recognized that the breakthrough to a new, indeed to the metalogical-dynamic method, to a new fundamental attitude of mind, is at stake here. For the carrying out of metalogic it follows from this, its prehistory, that it of course can express the dynamic of the elements of meaning in symbols that stem from the emotional side of consciousness. But it follows at the same time that the goal of this symbolism is the intuition of the forms of meaning filled with a living import, not the intuition of any sort of independent metaphysical essences. For the elements of meaning belong together; there is no import apart from a form, and no form without import. This antithesis of form and import obtains only for that intuiting of essences which perceives life and the relations of the forms of meaning through the manner in which they give expression to the import.

The inner dynamic of the forms of meaning, of the functions and categories, leads beyond philosophical considerations to cultural history, and then to the establishment of norms. The inner polarity of all forms of meaning makes possible a constructive understanding of the fulfillments of meaning realized in cultural history, and pushes on to the idea of a resolution of tension, not in an abstract manner, but in a creative solution of the problems brought to the fore by the spiritual process (*Geistesprozess*). The individual-creative element stemming from the pragmatic method finds its place here. It is the differentiation, made possible by the metalogical method between the concept of essence and the concept of norm, which provides it with access to this element, in contrast to the critical method. For in consequence of the lack of dynamic tension in pure criticism, it provides no methodological basis for a concrete concept of norm. On the contrary, formal criticism reduces the whole of reality to pure form and thus deprives the concrete forms of their significance.

A difficulty that obtains for the critical and the metalogical method alike has to do with nomenclature. The problem is how one can justify introducing a concept of essence (which has been developed only by means of the critical or the metalogical method) as the essence of particular phenomena that carry an already fixed name. How, for instance, can one methodologically justify giving the name "religion" [from ordinary usage] to a function of meaning independently established by the metalogical method? By force of the name given to it a function of meaning is presented as the essence of phenomena that through ordinary usage have been brought into a conceptual association. By means of the name given to them the concept of essence (which has been deduced through the critical method) and the universal concept in current usage are brought into connection with each other. The question now is, how is this relationship to be understood? For phenomenology, language provides access to the intuition of essences. To intuit the intention contained in a word is a basic demand of phenomenology. It is presupposed that the collectivity creating the language stands in intuitive unity with the essences, and that language therefore is an immediate revelation of essence. Metalogic can share this presupposition within certain limits. It can appreciate the claim that the creative spirit reveals itself in language. But by reason of its theory of individual creativity metalogic cannot admit that the "intentions" of language reveal essences as such. It can therefore concern itself with language in such a way that it not only understands the "intention" of the language but also alters it in the process. Metalogic stands in the living stream of meaning-realities, a stream that also includes the holy or religiously qualified realities. Only on the basis of the meaning-reality can metalogic accomplish its critical analysis; but it does not bind itself to fixed creations of this stream, not even to language. Rather, through a productive criticism of word and reality, it shapes new forms out of the stream.

Finally, we should observe that the relation between philosophy of religion and the empirical science of religion is also defined by the preceding considerations. After all that has been said, it should be clear that philosophy of religion cannot derive the concept of the essence of religion from the science of religion, but rather that such a concept is presupposed in all religious-scientific work. Hence, the relation has not been adequately described in these definitions. In a double direction the relations between empirical science and normative science go beyond these definitions. The empirical scientific clarification of actual conditions can certainly not be of any methodological significance for the critical-metalogical abstraction of the principles of meaning, and yet in actuality it is of great importance for it. On this account it has frequently become customary to place an empirical theory of the phenomena of religion ahead of the properly philosophical discussions. Against this procedure the following considerations must be taken into account. In every empirical science the empirical apprehension of religion is in ceaseless flux, and it is an almost impossible undertaking to develop from the provisional results of these empirical studies a systematic theory of the phenomena. At all events, it is impossible to base a philosophy of religion on such an *omnium gatherum;* on the contrary, this theory of the phenomena presupposes already a concealed or an openly operative concept of the essence of religion. And its development is neither methodologically nor even actually dependent upon the empirical science of religion. Empiricism can give much clarification, and thus it is possible that the religious principle of meaning can be derived from the immediately given, though not yet empirically analyzed, meaning-reality. Actually, the influence of the empirical science of religion is more direct upon the cultural history of religion than upon philosophy of religion. Although this is true, yet even in cultural history the empirical-historical problem as such is not touched: indeed, nonexistent "data" could also be taken up into the theory of the historical development of the concept of essence. In fact, however, history presents the great directions in which spiritual acts have actually developed; artificial constructions of these directions have no power to convince. Therefore empiricism provides the material for cultural history and prepares the ground upon which the creative concept of norm can be reared. Even here, however, the concept of essence whose comprehension is the first and basic task of philosophy of religion and the normative science of religion, is decisive.

PART ONE § THE ESSENCE OF RELIGION

——— §§§ ———

1. The Derivation of the Concept of the Essence of Religion

a. The Elements of Meaning and Their Relations

Every spiritual act is an act of meaning; regardless of whether the realistic theory of knowledge speaks of a meaning-receiving act or the idealistic theory of knowledge speaks of a meaning-bestowing act, or the metalogical method speaks of a meaning-fulfilling act; regardless therefore of how the relation between subject and object are thought of in the spiritual act, spirit is always [the medium for] the actualization of meaning (*Sinnvollzug*), and the thing intended by the spirit is a systematic interconnection of meaning. Meaning is the common characteristic and the ultimate unity of the theoretical and the practical sphere of spirit, of scientific and aesthetic, of legal and social structures. The spiritual reality in which the spirit-bearing form (*Gestalt*) lives and creates, is a meaning-reality. Hence, the theory of the structure of meaning-reality, i.e., philosophy, is the theory of the principles of meaning, and its first task is an analysis of meaning itself, a theory of the elements of meaning. Now it is of course a paradoxical enterprise to try to understand the meaning of meaning; one cannot trace back the concept of meaning to a higher concept, since every higher concept would itself be again a manifestation of meaning, but one can only try to develop metalogically the elements contained in, subordinate to, and ever present in every actualization of meaning.

There are three elements in any awareness of meaning. First, an awareness of the interconnection of meaning in which every separate meaning stands and without which it would be meaningless. Second, an awareness of the ultimate meaningfulness of the interconnection of meaning and, through that, of every particular meaning, i.e., the consciousness of an unconditioned meaning which is present in every particular meaning. Third, an awareness of the demand under which every particular meaning stands, the demand to fulfill the unconditioned meaning. The first element of meaning therefore is the awareness given in every act of meaning, an awareness of the universal interconnection of meaning, an awareness of the totality, an awareness of the "world." In all awareness of meaning a world-awareness is contained. But world-awareness is itself not the ultimate. Even the totality of meaning need not be meaningful, but rather could disappear, like every particular meaning, in the abyss (*Abgrund*) of meaninglessness, if the presupposition of an unconditioned meaningfulness were not alive in every act of meaning. This unconditionality of meaning is itself, however, not a meaning, but rather is the ground of meaning. If we include in the term "forms of meaning" all particularities of individual meaning and of all separate connections of meaning and even the universal connection of meaning, then in relation to the universal connection the unconditioned meaning may be designated as the import of meaning. By the import of meaning we therefore do not mean the import attaching to the significance of a particular consummation of meaning, but rather the meaningfulness that gives to every particular meaning its reality, significance, and essentiality. In this context the individual import is identical with the form of meaning. Later on we shall be concerned particularly with the question of forms, and then the distinction between individual form and individual import, or better, "content" (*Inhalt*), will become important.

The import of meaning has for the form of meaning on the one hand the significance of the ground of meaningfulness; on the other hand it functions over against the form as the demand for an unconditioned fulfillment in meaning, a demand with which only the complete or perfect connection of all meaning could comply— the unconditioned form. However, the unconditioned form of meaning is an idea contradictory to the relation of form and import. The meaningfulness of all meaning is the ground, but it is also the abyss of every meaning, even of an unconditioned form of meaning. The idea that in an unconditioned form of meaning all ground of meaning exhausts itself would abolish the inner infinity of meaning; it would not be able to get rid of the possibility that all meaning might sink into meaninglessness. The unconditioned meaningfulness of all meaning depends upon the awareness of the inexhaustibility of meaning in the ground of meaning. A complete unity, however, would be an exhaustion of the inner infinity of meaning. Nevertheless, the demand for this unity is present in every act of meaning; for only through the perfected unity of all meaning can meaning come to unconditioned realization, i.e., to form.

b. THE GENERAL DEFINITION OF THE ESSENCE OF RELIGION

In this view of the elements of meaning the fundamental principles of the philosophy of religion and of culture are given. They may be demonstrated in every particular sphere of meaning, in the theoretical as well as in the practical functions. However, one may also immediately recognize the way of grasping the elements which is at the basis of the religious and the cultural attitudes. If consciousness is directed toward the particular forms of meaning and their unity, we have to do with *culture;* if it is directed toward the unconditioned meaning, toward the import of meaning, we have *religion. Religion is directedness toward the Unconditional, and culture is directedness toward the conditioned forms and their unity.* These are the most general and formal definitions arrived at in philosophy of religion and philosophy of culture. But these definitions are inadequate. Form and import belong together; it is meaningless to posit the one without the other. Every cultural act contains the unconditioned meaning; it is based upon the ground of meaning; insofar as it is an act of meaning it is substantially religious. This becomes evident in the fact that it is directed toward the unity of form, that it must be subordinated to the unconditioned demand for unity of meaning. But it is not religious by intention. It is not toward the Unconditional as such that it is directed; and when it turns toward the unity of meaning it certainly does not do so with the consciousness that the unconditioned meaning surpasses even the totality of meaning, i.e., it does not do so with a consciously religious attitude. Culture as culture is therefore substantially, but not intentionally, religious. Conversely, the religious act cannot direct itself toward the unconditioned meaning except *through* the unity of the forms of meaning. For import without form cannot be the object of an act of meaning. From the point of view of its form every religious act is therefore a cultural act; it is directed toward the totality of meaning. But it is not by intention cultural; for it does not have in mind the totality of meaning, but rather the import of meaning, the unconditioned meaning. *In the cultural act, therefore, the religious is substantial; in the religious act the cultural is formal.* Culture is the sum total of all spiritual acts directed toward the fulfillment of particular forms of meaning and their unity. Religion is the sum total of all spiritual acts directed toward grasping the unconditioned import of meaning through the fulfillment of the unity of meaning. It is, therefore, characteristic of religion that the forms of meaning are for it something to be passed through, and this in the twofold sense of having both to penetrate and to leave behind at the same time. Culture, on the other hand, stops short in the particular units of meaning, and ultimately does not go beyond the unity of meaning in general.

The field in which culture and religion meet is the common directedness toward the unity of meaning. This is the critical point for philosophy of religion, the point where it is decided whether philosophy of religion penetrates through to religion at all, or whether it is content with equating a synthetic unification (*Abschluss*) of culture-consciousness with religion. The critical-dialectical method is especially endangered in this way. This danger appears in the fact that the more this method stresses the dialectical element, the more emphatically it is subject to the unconditioned demand and therefore pushes the dialectical process beyond every definite form. But it does not see that this whole process, like every particular form of meaning, stands under the No of the unconditioned meaning, and can only through this No receive at the same time a Yes of meaningfulness. For only that which is the abyss of meaning can at the same time be the ground of it. Everything else stands before the abyss of meaninglessness. Here we find the common defect of numerous forms of the speculative, the critical and the idealistic philosophies of religion. Even Hegel did not avoid it. In all these ways a mere unification of the philosophy of culture is achieved, a "synthesis of the world of spirits," and not that for which even the perfect synthesis must remain but a symbol, the absolute ground of meaning itself.

On the other hand, phenomenology and the supernatural method that has inner affinities with it overlook the fact that religion and culture come together in their directedness toward the synthesis of forms. They are consequently not able to clarify the relation between religion and culture. They oscillate between ranking the one above the other, putting the one over against the other, and refusing to define the relationship at all. The ranking of religion *above* culture makes religion into merely one of a series of meanings, and overlooks the fact that religion points to the ground and abyss of all meaning. The ranking of one *against* the other destroys the unity of meaning, and condemns religion or culture to meaninglessness. The refusal to define the relationship is impossible, since in every act of meaning the unity of all meaning is contained as an element, and the denial of unity of meaning must lead to ranking the one against the other and thus to meaninglessness. Even an original and extremely significant definition of the nature of religion such as that of Rudolph Otto suffers from this refusal to make a systematic definition of the relation between religion and culture—and this was not accidental in Otto's case, but rather was due to the phenomenological character of the method he adopted.

The metalogical method with its distinction between ground of meaning and unity of meaning is able to indicate at the same time the positive and the negative relations between religion and culture, and thus to present the religious function in its purity.

c. The Structure of the Functions of Meaning

Acts of meaning-fulfillment have a twofold character in that on the one hand they bring the immediately existing phenomenon to fulfillment through the spirit, and that on the other hand they themselves belong to the immediately existing things and accordingly are brought to fulfillment by other spiritual acts, for example, by historical interpretation. *Spirit* is always at the same time "material" for the fulfillment by meaning and the fulfillment itself. This twofoldness is manifest at the point where spiritual acts are rooted in being, namely, in the spirit-bearing Gestalt or in spiritual personality. This Gestalt on the one hand is the bearer of all meaning-fulfillment, and on the other its object. It is the place where what exists (*das Seiende*) achieves meaning. From this results a twofoldness in the functions of meaning: on the one hand those functions in which everything existing, even the spirit-bearing Gestalt itself, is taken up into fulfillment through meaning, and on the other those functions in which the spirit-bearing Gestalt detaches itself from its existential immediacy and establishes itself as a spiritual Gestalt. The first range of functions is the *theoretical,* the second the *practical.* The logical prius belongs to the practical range; for only insofar as the spirit-bearing Gestalt has submitted itself in its own being to the validity of form, can it in itself bring what exists to fulfillment. Actually, however, the one cannot obtain without the other. For a practical act is spiritual only when it carries in itself a theoretical awareness of the meaning and of the interconnections of its activity. Otherwise, it would remain an empty, futile act. Theoretical and practical acts therefore necessarily belong together; where either is missing, there can be no fulfillment in meaning. The theoretical act embraces reality in meaning; it is directed toward the form of things. For only in the interconnection of forms can the spirit-bearing Gestalt embrace being without breaking into pieces. The practical act shapes the spirit-bearing Gestalt into a personality. It is therefore directed toward the interconnections of being (Seins-zusammenhänge) in which the spirit-bearing Gestalt stands. For through the meaningful shaping of the interconnections of being the spirit-bearing Gestalt becomes personality. The theoretical act is the meaning-fulfillment in that aspect of it which is directly related to form. The practical act is the meaning-fulfillment of reality, insofar as reality is formed into spirit-bearing reality, through breaking loose from immediacy. The practical act is therefore meaning-fulfillment in the primary sense, and the theoretical act is fulfillment in the secondary sense. But for this reason the practical is limited to reality fulfilling itself in the spirit-bearing Gestalt, while the theoretical universally fulfills all reality in the ideal sphere. The practical is a real, the theoretical an ideal fulfillment in meaning.

The opposition of *real* and *ideal* is based on the double relationship of the import to the form of meaning. Insofar as the import of meaning comes to fulfillment in no form of meaning, but yet is the ground of every form of meaning, it becomes the material, the "matter," of meaning. *Matter* is the expression for the import of meaning viewed as detached from its unconditionedness and making possible particular contents of meaning. "Matter" as an absolute datum is a concept that is as impossible as perfect unity of form. For a "matter" given and self-contained in itself would be only one form among others, but not the infinite possibility of forms, as is demanded by the unconditionedness of the import of meaning. The genuine concept of "matter" has nothing to do with materiality in the sense of an objectification of the physical sphere of natural law; it expresses the basic originative, creative principle found in everything real, and reaches even into the sphere of the spirit-bearing *Gestalten*. A real meaning-fulfillment is one in which bestowal of meaning takes place in the sphere of individual reality bound to nature; an ideal fulfillment is one in which the giving of meaning involves no transformation in the material sphere, but rather a fulfillment of the existent thing in its immediate formation. The first, however, is possible only *in* the spiritual personality, the second only *by means of* it. Thus personality is the place of meaning-fulfillment, both real and ideal.

The indissoluble bond of ideal and real, of theoretical and practical, fulfillment in meaning has an effect in both directions of functioning through the influence of the one tendency upon the other, so that a duality arises in each of the functions. In the theoretical direction through the influence of the real sphere the artistic-aesthetic function establishes itself in distinction from the scientific-logical function. In ordinary linguistic usage the second of these has usurped the name "theoretical." As a matter of fact, both are theoretical, that is to say, intuiting or meaning-fulfilling in an ideal mode. The aesthetic is distinguished from the logical function only by the fact that in it a real meaning-fulfillment is given expression in the ideal sphere. The aesthetic shaping of things expresses that aspect of reality which is oriented to its import and which therefore makes possible a real connection with the spiritual personality. But this real connection remains only a possibility; it remains in the sphere of ideality, and from the logical point of view falls under the category of mere "appearance." This is the reason for the frequent but erroneous conception of the aesthetic

as a synthesis of the theoretical and the practical; in truth, however, the aesthetic remains in the ideal, i.e., the theoretical sphere.

In an analogous way the thereotical operates in the practical
order, and establishes the social sphere in distinction from the
sphere of law. Whereas in the sphere of law the structured relations
(*Seinsbeziehungen*) of spiritual personalities are interpreted in the
light of the meaning-fulfilling form, in the sphere of community a
fulfillment of these immediately developing structural relations
takes place. Consequently, both the cognition and the apprehension (or intuiting) of the import of life, elements that are co-
operative in every act of community-formation, have always been
evident, and have made it possible for love (as the highest symbol
of the social sphere) to become the all-embracing concept for the
theoretical and the practical (as, for example, in the idea of mystical
love). But the social is just as little a synthesis of the two spheres as
the aesthetic. The fundamentally practical quality of the social
remains primary.

With these details the structure of the spiritual realm has been
presented insofar as it is absolutely necessary for the philosophy
of religion. It is now possible to show how the same elements of
meaning from which we have derived the basic concept of religion
are also contained in the theoretical and practical functions. We
turn now accordingly to set forth the religious dimension in the
separate functions of the spirit.

d. The Religious Dimension in the Various Functions of
Meaning

In every act of knowing is contained the knowing process and
that which is known, the meaning-fulfilling directedness and the
material of meaning-fulfillment—*thought* and *being*. In the act of
knowing, both have become one by concealing an infinite inner

tension, a tension that remains unresolved even in the completed act of knowledge. Thought aims to become one with being. But it can never completely absorb being into itself. Otherwise, thought would become empty and meaningless. It must recognize the infinite transcendence of all being over against thought. Precisely in this transcendence of being in face of thought rests the reality of every cognitive claim. Without this transcendence, being would be dissolvable in thought. At the same time the transcendence of being expresses itself in the infinite demand contained in every act of thought to state truth, i.e., to be a necessary member in the totality of the logical claims through which thought apprehends being. We find therefore in any particular stance of the knowing act on the one hand an awareness of the infinite reality of all being, striving as it does against thought and at the same time providing a basis for thought, and on the other hand the demand for a universal knowledge of being, a demand driving out beyond the particular, the individual. It is now possible for the spirit to orient itself to the infinity of the particular claims to knowledge and their achieved unity, or to the unconditioned being that is the basis for everythng particular and yet transcends everything particular. The first directedness is the cultural one, the second the religious. In the sphere of knowledge culture is directedness toward the conditioned forms of existence and their unity. Religion in the sphere of knowledge is directedness toward the unconditionally existing (*das unbedingt Seiende*) as the ground and abyss of all particular claims and their unity.

In the aesthetic sphere the elements of meaning stand in the same relation to one another. In all aesthetic shaping an essential import (*Wesensgehalt*) is supposed to be brought to expression. The forms that are employed in aesthetic intuition have nothing to do with logical validity. They do not express apprehensions of being, but rather of what is significant. But every thing and every process has *significance* (*Bedeutung*) through its relation to the unconditioned ground of significance and through being part of a universal interconnection of significance. The significance of the real as apprehended in aesthetic feeling never remains attached to a particular significance and is never to be apprehended through empirical emotional states. The unconditioned significance pulsates in and through every aesthetic experience, and every aesthetic feeling is a transcendent feeling, that is, one in which the empirical emotional agitation includes a kernel of experience pointing to the Unconditional. Directedness toward particular significances and their interconnections in the uinversal work of art is the cultural-aesthetic act. Directedness toward the unconditioned import of significance and its presentation in the universal interconnection of significance is religion.

In the sphere of law (*Recht*) it is a question of creating such patterns of order that the relation of the spiritual personality to other personalities and to subpersonal reality corresponds to the nature of the spirit-bearing personal life. The relation of the personal, however, to every immediately existing reality (and both the other personality and one's own psychophysical organization are existing realities) is the relation of freedom. All forms of law are forms through which the freedom of the person is made possible. The recognition of the free personality is inherent in every legal axiom as an unconditionally valid idea. The unconditionedness of the personal is the supporting ground of all consciousness of what is just. In every act of this consciousness is contained on the one hand the awareness of the unconditionally personal as the meaning-ground of all law. On the other hand, this consciousness implies the demand for an unconditioned actualization of the right, i.e., for the universal unity of justice. Thus every act of the

legal consciousness contains at one and the same time an awareness of the unconditioned meaning-ground of everything just and
right, and the awareness of the unconditioned form of the right
which sublates every particular right. The intention of the spirit
toward a particular legal form and the ideal unity of forms, viewed
apart from the meaning-ground of all right which transcends every
particular right, is the cultural attitude of culture. The intention of
the spirit toward the unconditionally personal as the ground of
every right and the implementation of this intention in a kingdom
of righteousness is the religious attitude.

In the pure sphere of law the relation of personalities to one
another is defined by justice, *i.e.*, by the acknowledgement of the
other as being a free personality. This relation among personalities, however, is not the only one. The immediate community
stands beside it as the living import of personality relationships,
and *love* is the universal meaning-fulfilling form of that community. All immediate forms of community are forms of love. But
like the aesthetic forms, these forms have the quality of significance (*Bedeutung*). They express an import, but apart from it
they have no rational, in this case therefore no legal, meaning;
they can only be understood by grasping the import attaching to
their significance but not by giving them a place in a legal framework. With respect to both the community function and law, however, it must be said that the presupposition of an unconditioned
love is contained in every act of spiritual, hence of meaning-fulfilling, love. As the unconditioned import of significance pulsates in
the aesthetic intuition of any one particular significance, so the
unconditioned meaning of love, "the love of love," is present in all
spiritual love. At the same time, however, the meaning-fulfilling
act of community contains the unconditioned demand for a universal community of love from which nothing is excluded. The inner

directedness toward the particular forms of the realization of love and their unity is the cultural attitude in the sphere of community; the inner directedness toward unconditioned love (which at the same time is the ground as well as the abyss of any particular love) and toward the universal unity of love as its symbol, is the religious attitude.

Thus, corresponding to the universal apprehension of the religious within the very nature of meaning itself, it has become evident that religion is immanent in all the functions of meaning, theoretical as well as practical. The twofold method of derivation from both the theoretical and the practical is of decisive importance for the apprehension of the Unconditional. The merely theoretical way makes the Unconditional into an object which, like any other object, can be manipulated or disposed of by the personality. But as a consequence it loses the power of unconditionedness. It can retain this power only through the [correction provided by the] practical side that makes the recognition of the unconditionally personal into an unconditionally personal demand. But conversely, the merely practical way loses the Unconditional in its quality of grounding and at the same time transcending everything real; it makes the Unconditional into a mere demand without presence. Thus, it also loses the character of unconditionedness and is changed into a product of unconditioned action. Only if it views the Unconditional as that which exists unconditionally in all of being can it preserve the element of unconditionedness. The two ways must supplement each other, and only together in their unity do they provide the living apprehension of the unconditioned meaning that constitutes the ground and abyss of all meaning.

e. The Nature and Truth of Religion

It has become customary to subdivide the philosophy of religion into the double question concerning the *nature* and *truth* of religion. Where this division occurs, however, the method of the philosophy of religion has not yet been perfected. The distinction between the question as to the nature and the question as to the truth of religion depends upon a combination of empirical and speculative methods. First, the nature of religion is established empirically, and then its truth is established speculatively. This implies, however, on the one hand—apart from the methodological impossibility of the empirical method—the conception of religion as an act which would be equally possible whether or not its object existed. On the other hand—apart from the unfeasibility of the speculative proof—a religious object is sought after which is detached from the religious act. This tearing apart of the act and the object of the act is the basic defect of many philosophies of religion; thus the way is obstructed for the apprehension of religion as an independent function, that is, the way to the philosophy of religion. The metalogical method does not admit this dualism; for it the questions concerning the nature and truth of religion are identical. In the proof that the religious function is the grounding function of meaning, a proof of the nature and truth of religion and an indication of the act and the object of the act are immediately given. It is the superiority of the metalogical method that it apprehends the truth along with the nature of religion, and that it is not necessary for it to prove the truth of religion from outside religion, neither speculatively, nor morally, nor through the ethical evaluation of religious witnesses, nor pragmatically. The question concerning the truth of religion is answered by the metalogical apprehension of the nature of religion as directedness toward the unconditioned meaning. It is meaningless to ask beyond that whether the Unconditional "exists," hence whether the religious act is oriented to something real and in that respect is true or not. For the question whether the Unconditional exists presupposes already the unconditioned meaningfulness inherent in every act of knowing; it presupposes that which exists unconditionally. The certainty of the Unconditional is the grounding certainty from which all doubt can proceed, but it can never itself be the object of doubt. Therefore the object of religion is not only real, but is also the presupposition of every affirmation of reality. But it is not real in the sense of some particular affirmation. Moreover, the universal synthesis is not something "given," but rather a symbol. In the true symbol, reality is apprehended; but a symbol is an improper form of expression which is always necessary where a proper expression is in the nature of things impossible. The symbolic character of religious ideas in no way deprives them of their reality, but it lifts this reality out of the conditioned into the unconditioned, that is, into the religious, sphere. The intention to speak unsymbolically of religion is irreligious, for it deprives the Unconditional of its unconditionality and leads to a rightful rejection, as a creature of fantasy, of this Unconditional which has been thus transformed into an object.

In the metalogical apprehension of the nature of religion the question regarding the truth of religion also finds an answer: the sphere of meaning having to do with truth, like all spheres of meaning, finds its ground in the unconditioned meaning intended in religion. The question as to truth has in general first gained a meaning only on the ground of the religious. The questions as to the essence and the truth of religion converge.

An objection against the merging of these two questions cannot be supported by claiming that the functions of meaning are the starting point for the analysis of essence, and that the objectivity of the intention is by no means demonstrated by the mere apprehension of the intention of meaning. The objection proceeds from a subjectively idealistic interpretation of the functions of meaning; but subjective idealism is precluded by the concept of meaning-fulfillment. It is not the function as a function that is analyzed but rather the meaning coming to fulfillment in it, a meaning that lies beyond the opposition of function and object. Analyses of meaning are analyses of being, because meaning brings being to spiritual fulfillment. This comes to expression in the analyses themselves by virtue of the fact that every act of meaning is related to the unconditioned meaning viewed as an abyss of meaning. While the merely critical method, which adheres only to the forms of meaning, is exposed to the criticism directed against subjective idealism, it belongs to the nature of the metalogical method to break through every such subjectivity and [in the philosophy of religion] to resolve the problem of reality. From this point of view it should be stressed again that the analysis of the essence of the religious according to the metalogical method requires no supplementation by a proof of the truth of religion; indeed, it contains within itself the solution of "the problem of reality" for all the spheres of meaning.

2. The Essential Elements of Religion and Their Relations

a. RELIGION AND CULTURE

Religion is directedness of the spirit toward the unconditioned meaning. Culture is directedness of the spirit toward conditioned forms. Both, however, meet in orientation to the completed unity of the forms of meaning. This unity is for culture the capstone, but for religion it is a symbol. From the point of view of the Unconditional this symbol is at the same time affirmed and negated; this is the general outcome of the metalogical analysis of meaning. Religion, therefore, is not one meaning-function alongside others. This follows immediately from its character as directedness toward the Unconditional. That which is the basis of all functions of meaning cannot itself be one of these functions. Rather, the relation is such that the meaning-functions come to fulfillment in meaning only in relatedness to the unconditioned meaning, and that therefore the religious intention is the presupposition for successful meaning-fulfillment in all functions. An assertion of existence which is not directed toward that which exists unconditionally, an apprehension of significance not directed toward the ground of significance, a shaping of the personality not directed toward the unconditionally personal, a spiritual act of love not directed toward unconditioned love, cannot be recognized as a successful meaning-fulfillment. Only in the "Holy Spirit" does the nature of spirit find its realization. It comes to realization, however, not in forms that stand alongside the cultural ones (through which the unconditionedness of religion would be dissolved) but rather precisely in the cultural forms; culture is a form of expression of religion, and religion is the substance (*Inhalt*) of culture. With these sentences the provisional co-ordination of the initial derivation is again dissolved; we have gone a full circle through which the cultural element, the system of meaning-functions which was first in the derivation, has moved to second place.

It is only in a preliminary way, therefore, that the philosophy of religion takes as its starting point the functions of meaning. This procedure serves to show that the meaning-functions, in their being and their meaning, are grounded in the religious, that they are forms that become meaningless and without import as soon as they lose the intention toward the unconditioned import of meaning. This outcome, however, corresponds to the demand of religion itself. It is the solution of the basic problem in the philosophy of religion: philosophical analysis is driven to the point where it apprehends itself together with all of culture as an expression of the religious.

The unity of religion and culture as a unity of unconditioned meaning-import and of conditioned meaning-form is the authentic relation of the two. We call this unity theonomy, and we understand by that word the fulfillment of all cultural forms with the import of the Unconditional. But now the question must be raised, under what presuppositions can there be a co-ordination (*Nebenordnung*) of culture and religion? And what consequences follow from this for both sides? The philosophy of religion does indeed begin from such a coordination, and it reveals the essential unity only through the metalogical analysis of meaning. Now, since we have recognized the preliminary character of this procedure, we must reverse our course, and start anew from the achieved goal of the theonomous unity, in order eventually to understand the situation out of which the problem of the philosophy of religion arises.

Culture is directedness toward the conditioned forms of meaning and their fulfillment. In this definition a separation of culture and religion is not yet indicated; for the fulfillment in meaning of all forms lies in the unconditioned meaning. Yet the possibility of a separation is indicated, the possibility that the spirit will relate itself to the conditioned forms and their unity without paying heed to the unconditioned meaning, and therefore without bringing to expression the critical judgment of the Unconditional against the unity of meaning. It is the absolutizing of the conditioned that gives rise to the separation of culture from religion. In contrast to theonomy, we call this autonomy. In every autonomy—that is, in every secular culture—a twofold element is implied: the "nomos," the law or structural form that is supposed to be carried out radically, corresponding to the unconditioned demand for meaning, and the "autos," the self-assertion of the conditioned, which in the process of achieving form loses the unconditioned import. Autonomy therefore is always at the same time obedience to and revolt against the Unconditional. It is obedience insofar as it subjects itself to the unconditioned demand for meaning; it is revolt insofar as it denies the unconditioned meaning itself. Autonomous culture is, as the myth puts it, always at the same time *hybris* and a gift of the god.

In face of autonomy religion takes refuge in particular symbols which it exempts from autonomous criticism and to which it ascribes unconditionedness and inviolability. The unconditioned meaning is supposed to be apprehended in certain particular forms, and is to reveal itself in a specifically religious sphere. The other forms remain left over to the autonomous culture, but only under the presupposition that the religious symbols are acknowledged as unconditionally authoritative. This counterattitude to autonomy is heteronomy. It rises against the *hybris* of autonomy, and submits itself to the unconditioned meaning; but it does not understand the divinely ordained character of autonomy, namely, the apprehension of the pure forms and their unity. It falls victim therefore to religious *hybris*, the counterpole of cultural *hybris*.

Autonomy and heteronomy live from theonomy and fall to pieces as soon as the theonomous synthesis has entirely disappeared. Autonomy without the import of the Unconditional becomes empty and without power of life and creativity. Likewise, heteronomy without autonomous consciousness of form is spiritually impossible; it loses its power of conviction and becomes a demonic means of power contrary to meaning, until it breaks down.

Autonomy and heteronomy are tensions within theonomy,

which can lead to a breaking asunder and thus to the catastrophe of the spirit, for the essential relation of culture and religion is theonomy. Every philosophy of religion is to be reproached which proceeds from only one of the two poles, without coming to the synthesis and correcting the defect of the one-sided starting point.

b. Faith and "Unfaith"

Directedness toward the Unconditional, of which we have spoken in connection with the derivation of the concept of the nature of religion, we call *faith*. Faith is a turning toward the Unconditional, effective in all functons of the spirit. Faith, therefore, is not identical with any one of the other functions, neither with the theoretical, as a frequent misunderstanding supposes, nor with the practical, as the opposing conception contends. Faith is not the acceptance of uncertain objects as true; it has nothing to do with acceptance or probability. Nor is it merely the establishing of a community relationship, like confidence or obedience or the like; rather, it is the apprehension of the Unconditional as the ground of both the theoretical and the practical. But faith is also no special function alongside other functions. It comes to expression only in them, and is their root. There is a belief-ful theoretical and practical behavior, but there is no belief-ful behavior as such. Every act of faith is an embracing or shaping turn toward the Unconditional. Faith is neither mere *assensus,* nor mere *fiducia.* But in every belief-ful *assensus* there is *fiducia,* and in every belief-ful *fiducia* there is *assensus.*

Faith is directedness toward the Unconditional in the theoretical and the practical act. The Unconditional as such, however, can never be an object but only the *symbol* in which the Unconditional is intuited and intended. Faith is orientation to the Unconditional

76

through symbols drawn from the conditioned order. Every act of faith therefore has a double meaning. It is directed immediately toward a holy object. It does not, however, intend this object, but rather the Unconditional which is symbolically expressed in the object. Faith reaches beyond the immediacy of all things to the ground and abyss upon which they depend.

In contrast to faith we have the unbelief-ful attitude. Its essence is not that it fails to recognize or to accomplish something or other that is objective; rather, its essence is that it stops with the actualities or objects in their immediacy, in their conditioned forms, and does not penetrate through to the grounding import. Unbelief-fulness is therefore the mark of the typically autonomous attitude of culture; but it is that only by intention. Actually, every creative cultural act is also belief-ful; in it pulsates the meaning of the Unconditional. Otherwise, it would in the end be without meaning and without import. But the cultural intention as an intention is unbelief-ful. It is that even when it is directed toward religious symbols; for it does not intend the Unconditional that shatters every symbol, but rather it intends the unity of the conditioned. It remains preoccupied with the world even when it speaks of God. God is for it a synthesis of immanental forms, but not the abyss of the world. The dialectic of autonomous culture, therefore, is that it lives in faith so long as it is creative (even if it fights against the religious symbols, for example, "the existence of God") while it nevertheless is unbelief-ful with respect to intention (even though it accepts the religious symbols, for example, proves the "existence of God").

In contrast to autonomous unbelief-fulness, religion seeks to protect from autonomous criticism the particular forms that have attained symbolic significance. It gives to them a heteronomous validity and turns faith into a form-shattering act. Faith is no longer directedness toward the Unconditional through conditioned forms, rather it is directedness toward conditioned forms viewed as unconditioned. Heteronomous faith also stops with the conditioned form, only it does not interpret it as conditioned—as does autonomous "unfaith"—but rather as a bearer of the Unconditional. Heteronomous faith is faith, even though it is demonically distorted (see below), while autonomous "unfaith" is never demonic, but also never divine; rather, it is empty obedience to law (*Gesetz*).

With this insight into the essence of faith the problems of "faith and knowledge" and "faith and works" are solved. Both problems arise from the opposition of autonomy and heteronomy, and both are solved in theonomy. Faith is not a cognition or an action that may stand alongside autonomous cognition and action with heteronomous claim to absoluteness. Just as little is it a cognition or action that could be grounded in autonomous cognition or action. Rather it is directedness toward the unconditioned meaning-import, operative in both and grounding both. Faith is the prius of cognition and of meaning-fulfilled action. Cognition and action without faith are empty and without reality. A faith, however, which through the recognition of a definite form is supposed to be grounded in cognition and action, is a law·that is incapable of fulfillment, which destroys truthfulness and love, and therefore leads to compromise or to despair. The Reformation emancipated man from the law of action in late-Catholic heteronomy; but in accord with the spiritual situation, it left the "law" of cognition untouched and inviolable. Modern Protestantism has freed man from the law of cognition, but has led into the emptiness of un-belief-ful autonomy. The meaning of a coming theonomy would be this: to be belief-ful in [and through] the autonomous form of knowledge and action.

c. God and World

In the objective sphere the duality of religion and culture, of faith and "unfaith," finds a parallel in the duality of God and the world. In a metalogical philosophy of religion one can speak of God only insofar as he is intended in a religious act. An extrareligious speaking of God contradicts the methodological as well as the material presuppositions. God is the object intended in faith, and beyond that nothing. This, however, is not to say that the object is as it were to be made into a product of the subject, as though God were a creation of faith. Rather, faith as faith is determined by its directedness toward the Unconditional; and the reality of the Unconditional is the foundation of every assertion regarding reality. But the act of grasping the Unconditional is an act of faith; without faith the Unconditional is not apprehensible.

The act of faith realizes itself in theoretical and practical acts; both presuppose a concrete object to which they are directed. But the Unconditional is no concrete object. By means of objects it can only be symbolized, but not apprehended. The object of faith necessarily has a symbolic character; it intends more than it expresses. Whether a sacred stone or a personal omnipotent Spirit is believed in, the intention of faith always transcends the object of faith. In the abyss of the Unconditional the one as well as the other disappears. Not the unbeliever, but rather the believer [the belief-ful person] is the real atheist, and in every genuine theism, in every affirmation of God as the Unconditional, an abyss of atheism is contained—the affirmation is again sublated. "God" is the symbol for the Unconditional; but it is a symbol, exactly as faith as an act is a symbolic act (here faith is not viewed as the ground and abyss of the act). God is not only his own ground but also his own abyss. Corresponding to the presence of the unconditional meaning-import in all of being, every existing thing can become a symbol of the Unconditional. But corresponding to the unconditioned demand of the form of meaning, a perfect symbol of the Unconditional is only the completed unity of meaning: the synthesis of the existent and its significance in unity, together with the synthesis of the personal and its fullness. Logical and aesthetic, legal and social, in short, metaphysical and ethical intentions, come together in this symbol. It is to be grasped neither as a theoretical object nor as a practical idea, but rather only as a unity of both. This synthesis of syntheses is the highest, always-intended symbol of the Unconditional.

The absolute synthesis, however, is not necessarily a symbol of the Unconditional. Looked at in an immediate way it is the unity of the conditioned order; but as a unity of the conditioned order it is the *world*. The same idea can therefore have an immediate and a symbolic, a religious and a cultural, significance; it can be God and the world. A concept like the Hegelian "absolute Spirit" is in an immediate way the synthesis of world-forms, but it can symbolically signify God. It is now of decisive importance for philosophy of religion and theology, to grasp this difference in all its sharpness.

Unbelief-ful autonomy stops with the synthesis of world-forms and asserts its immediate identity with God. It dissolves the "abyss in God," the divine-creative in which also the demonic is contained, and does not see the negativities of the Unconditional in face of the synthesis of forms, the world. Unbelief-ful autonomy is idealism; and it is a necessary historical fate that a realism follows it in which the subterranean demonic elements of the world swallow up the synthesis of forms. The dissolution of God into the world has for its inevitable consequence the destruction of the consciousness of the world as mere world. For the synthesis of the world-forms depends upon the unconditioned ground and abyss of meaning. The consciousness of the world as world is a product of the consciousness of God, and in its permanency is dependent upon the latter.

Belief-ful heteronomy, on the other hand, makes the ground and abyss of reality into a reality of its own above the world. The truth that the Unconditional grounds being and significance, personality and love, is transformed and perverted into the untruth that the Unconditional is all this in an objective sense. God becomes a world alongside the world. He is not intended as a world, but he becomes that with dialectical necessity; and since the unity of form resides in the nature of the world, the autonomous world-consciousness is shattered. On the other hand, the Unconditional receives the quality of the world, it becomes an object and a form of its own which stands beside the world, and it cannot be freed from this "beside" arrangement by any pious appeal to a "super-world," no matter how strenuous the attempt.

Theonomy uncovers and identifies the inwardly dialectical character of the concept of God. It reaches beyond the synthesis of world-forms to the ground and abyss of the world which is neither innerworldly nor otherworldly but rather breaks through the completed world-form and yet is never a form of its own alongside the world.

d. The Sacred and the Secular

A meaning-fulfilling act or an object of meaning is sacred insofar as it is a bearer of the unconditional meaning; it is secular insofar as it does not give expression to the unconditional meaning. In the ideal theonomy every meaning-reality and every act of meaning is sacred. But perfected theonomy is the perfected kingdom of God, that is, it is a symbol and not a reality. Reality is pervaded by the tensions between the sacred and the secular and by the ruptures of these tensions, that is, either by the disjunction of the sacred and the secular or by creative forms of adjustment which point toward a perfect theonomy. In reality there is a specifically sacred sphere that stands over against the sphere of the secular.

The relation of the unconditional to the conditioned meaning is the crucial criterion for the appearance of the sacred or the Holy, the relation that we have characterized by the double symbol "ground" and "abyss." From the vantage point of the Unconditional the affirmation and the negation of the existent [*Seiende*] are contained in every sacred reality [*Sein*]. There is an affirmation in the sense that the existent reality is supported in its depth by an import absolutely transcending all particular reality; from this import the finite, like all reality, acquires its true nature, meaning and significance. At the same time there is a negation in the sense that it is not its appearance as such that gives the existent reality this quality, but rather that its appearance, like the appearance of everything real, is absolutely negated from the perspective of the Holy. The sacred object is therefore never holy in itself but rather only through a negation of itself; and this negation of itself includes the negation of everything existent. Every sacred reality becomes the vessel of the duality of absolute fulfillment through meaning and the absolute abyss of meaning. Both, however, stand in absolute contrast to the immediate reality (*Sein*) of the thing, to its character as a particular form in the universal interconnection of forms. The Holy breaks through the immediate form of the existent; it possesses ecstatic qualities. Every holy reality (*Sein*) is an ecstatic reality, that is, one that bursts through its immediately given formation; it has an inner transcendence reaching beyond its formal, cultural givenness. This holds for the subjective sphere of every act of faith, whether the latter expresses itself in personal prayer or in the consciousness-dissolving transport of mystical ecstasy. It holds also in the objective sphere of every symbol of the divine, whether it be that of the personal God abiding upon his depths, or the horrifying figures of the gods of India.

There are three ways to interpret the inner ecstatic quality of the Holy. From the point of view of heteronomy the Holy is the supernatural; for autonomy it is the ideal; for theonomy it is the paradoxical. Supernaturalism asserts that the Holy has so far united itself with the sacred object or event that the latter is raised as a whole into a higher sphere and stands over against everything else (which is viewed as something secular). In this way the insight is lost, that the sacredness of the holy reality (*Sein*) issues from the negation of its immediate existence (*Dasein*) and that by this fact it is actually in the same situation with everything else secular. Idealism, on the other hand, aims to transcend the immediate givenness by means of the ideal demand. It makes ecstasy into enthusiasm for the ideal; it does not see that even the immediately existing thing has its ground in the Unconditional, nor does it see that even the ideal reality (*Sein*) is negated by the Unconditional. Idealism forgets the "ground" in considering the thing as it is and the "abyss" in considering the thing as it ought to be. Theonomy, which ideally sees the Holy in all forms, must reject supernaturalism because the latter sanctifies a particular form in and for itself, and thereby excludes all other forms; and it must reject idealism because it no longer places the ideal forms, theoretical or practical, under the No of the Unconditional, and thus improperly desecrates the real forms and sanctifies the ideal forms. Theonomy itself uncovers and identifies the paradoxical character of the Holy and of ecstasy, the inner transcending character, the quality of breaking through immediate forms and of interpreting them symbolically. As against both supernaturalism and idealism it thus achieves the insight that the state of holiness is *grace,* and not a supernatural sphere, but also not a merely natural ideal demand. Grace is always a paradox; it breaks through the immediate form but has no form of its own.

Things therefore do not themselves possess the ground of their sacredness. They are not holy in themselves. Yet there are things and persons, forms and events, that have a superior symbolic power whose meaning-fulfillment it is to become sacred things. Often this possibility does not depend upon the intrinsic quality of these phenomena but rather upon a fateful coincidence through which objects that in themselves are relatively lacking in symbolic power receive an extraordinary symbolic power from the subjective side. The universal mark of symbolic powerfulness is the ecstatic quality, the being imbued with the import of the Unconditional which a thing has or through subjective intention receives. This universal mark can make itself evident in a variety of ways. The symbolic power, however, always disappears as soon as a thing is entirely integrated into the framework of cultural forms, in short, as soon as it has been entirely secularized. Therefore the autonomous approach to things, which integrates them from the point of view of an ideal unity, leads to the secularization of the Holy, while heteronomy aims to preserve the holiness of the fatefully sanctified thing and exalts it supernaturally above the formal interconnection of meaning. Both, however, contradict the paradoxical character of the Holy.

By virtue of the fact that the Holy transcends positively and negatively all immediate forms of consciousness, it becomes for consciousness on the one hand the fulfillment toward which the latter strives, and on the other the abyss before which it recoils;

and both of these are united. The first makes the Holy into something that blesses man, that is, into that wherein consciousness finds its unconditional fulfillment; the second makes the Holy into the Inviolable which the secular consciousness should not approach. The first comes to clearest expression in the hymns of blessedness of the mystics, the second in the "tabu," the plastic symbol of the negative unconditionedness of the Holy. From the first come all attempts within religion to achieve perfection within the Unconditional and the Holy through union with sacred things and through ecstatic states of consciousness. From the second come all ideas of purification and emptying, that is, of eliminating the secular elements of consciousness without whose negation it is not possible to become a vessel for the reception of grace.

e. The Divine and the Demonic

In the sphere of the Holy itself there arises the polarity of the divine and the demonic. The demonic is the Holy (or the sacred) with a minus sign before it, the sacred antidivine. The possibility of the demonic resides in the peculiar relation of form and import: the inexhaustibility of the import of meaning signifies on the one hand the meaningfulness of every form of meaning, and on the other it presupposes the endless resistance of matter to form. That which is meaning-supporting is through its inner infinity therefore at the same time hostile to meaning. In the sphere of the spiritual fulfillment through meaning the resistance of the material becomes a positive hostility to meaning; it becomes "sin." The spiritual involves a dialectic, on the one hand to become actualized in being and thereby to participate in the infinite resistance of the material, on the other to stand as spirit under the unconditional demand, that is, to be free. Thus the immediate resistance of matter to form becomes in the sphere of the spirit, guilt. The demonic is a meaning-resistant thrust of matter which assumes the quality of the Holy. It can assume this quality, for it is an expression of the abyss of meaning; therefore it has also ecstatic qualities, as does the Holy of positive character. It is a breakthrough in the direction of the destructive, but a breakthrough that comes out of the same abyss as the breakthrough in the direction of grace. The difference, however, is this, that grace breaks through the form while both acknowledging the form and affirming the unconditional form, whereas the demonic does not submit to the unconditional form. The demonic has all the forms of expression that obtain for the sacred, but it has them with the mark of opposition to the unconditional form, and with the intention of destruction. The holy negativity of the abyss becomes demonic negativity through the loss of the unconditional form. The demonic, however, resides just as little as the divine in the intrinsic character of things in themselves. The supernaturalistic interpretation is to be rejected; likewise to be rejected is the idealistic interpretation, according to which the demonic is a falling short of the ideal form. Demonic possession, like blessedness or being possessed of grace, is a paradox; and, like the latter, it is evident in exceptionally symbolically powerful phenomena. It is no less decisive for a religious situation how it views the demonic than how it views the divine. Religion even creates a focal symbol of the demonic: the anti-god. In this symbol it unites the synthesis of the existent with the synthesis of the personal, as in the symbol of the divine, but here with a negative signature. Thus, to be sure, it runs into an inner contradiction insofar as every particular form that cannot be fitted into the universal form can be demonic; yet the universal form itself cannot be so, for it is what absolutely ought to be. Religious-metaphysical dualism in religion is untenable, even in the moderate form of the theory of the devil; the demonic is a principle, but not an idea. It is possible only in contradiction to the universal idea, that is, only in the particular. But as a principle it has the reality of the Holy itself.

The consciousness of the demonic presupposes a split in the awareness of God, the reason for this split being the hidden operation of autonomous form. While in the undifferentiated religious consciousness the demonic and the divine, the negativity of the abyss and the unconditioned ground of meaning are identical, in the consciousness that has become split God the bearer of meaning struggles against God the bearer of hostility to meaning. Thus, for example, ecstatic human sacrifice, all the way from primitive cannibalism to the highest asceticism, has been forced step by step into consciousness of the demonic, and Moloch has been stamped as the symbol of the demonic. The affirmation of the personal and the social on the part of religion has revealed the sacred undifferentiated form in its character of hostility to meaning, and has designated it as demonic.

As a consequence of the polarity between the divine and the demonic in the sphere of the Holy, the concept of the Holy itself becomes dialectical. The Holy in the original conception does not distinguish between the divine and the demonic. As soon, however, as the cleavage in the religious consciousness identifies the demonic as demonic, the concept of the Holy is identified with the divine. By the same token, the Holy becomes the righteous, the demanded. This development is reflected most clearly in the concept of religious purity (the "clean"). The Holy in the sense of "tabu," of the inviolable, the dangerous, is at the same time the unclean, over against which the secular is pure. With the division of the Holy into the divine and the demonic the concept of the unclean remains attached to the demonic, while the divine appears now as the pure. The Holy in the sense of the divine and the secular are therefore simultaneously subsumed under the category of the pure. Divine and secular alike stand over against the demonic. In common they affirm form, in contrast to the demonic which shatters it.

3. The Cultural History and Normative Concept of Religion

a. THE BASIC RELIGIOUS TENDENCIES

From the polarity between the divine and the demonic the basic religious tendencies can be derived, and also the cultural-historical "construction" of the history of religion. In general of course it is true that an element of the essence of religion is present in every religious phenomenon. Therefore in every form of religion the unity of form and import must be found. This unity is not only the ideal goal but also the essential presupposition of religious development. The difference, however, is this, that the unity of form and import as a point of departure is indifferent to the division of the Holy into the divine and the demonic, while the unity of form and import as the end-point has eliminated the demonic, or rather has integrated it into the divine. The movement from the point of departure to the end-point is therefore propelled by the struggle of the divine against the demonic. Naturally, starting-point and end-point are meant here only in an ideal sense and not chronologically. They are constructs and not realities. The reality lies between them, but in such a way that it is through their inner dialectic always pushed from one point to the other, in progress or regress.

Through the antidemonic influence of form the original undifferentiatedness bifurcates into the polarity of two basic attitudes, one of which we shall call the sacramental and the other the theocratic tendency. The sacramental attitude is laid hold of by criticism at the hands of form insofar as it is no longer able to intuit the Holy undifferentiatedly in everything real, but instead considers particular realities and forms as bearers of the holy import. These things and actions thereby receive a sacramental quality. Their significance depends upon the fact that in them, as finite, conditioned realities, the presence of the unconditioned import of meaning is experienced.

At the opposite pole from the sacramental is the theocratic tendency. It is the bearer of antidemonic criticism. We call it theocratic—in a slight deviation from ordinary usage—because it wishes to subject the forms of reality in action and knowledge to the unconditioned form, to obedience to the divine. In itself it has nothing to do with priestly domination, but it can be distorted into it. Theocracy turns against the deification of special sacramental realities. It demands obedience to the unconditioned form that critically negates every particular form. Theocracy is imbued with the struggle against all holy demonries connected with the sacramental. It wants to establish the sovereignty of God. But just as there is a theocratic element in the sacramental, so there is a sacramental element in the theocratic. The holy demand, if it is to be concrete, must issue from a sacred bearer, a mediator of revelation, who now on account of his theocratic power receives a sacramental consecration. From this sacramental element of theocracy new demonries can develop which lead to new theocratic reactions or to an autonomous dissolution.

On the soil of the basic sacramental attitude the dissolution of the sacramental can lead to a phenomenon that belongs among the most controversial elements in cultural history, namely, mysticism. Recently the attempt has been made to classify mysticism as a basic type of religion and to view it in contrast to prophetic religion. But this opposition is inadequately conceived. The prophetic is a much too narrow characterization of the theocratic, although it is true that the prophetic as a critical movement is to be associated with the theocratic. The great powerful theocratic movements are borne by prophetic personalities. But the essence of theocracy is by no means exhausted in this way.

On the other hand, mysticism is by no means a separate basic attitude. "Mysticism" means union with the unconditioned import of meaning as the ground and abyss of everything conditioned. In this sense mysticism is essential to all religion. For orientation to the unconditioned ground of meaning is an essential element of religion. Mysticism as a special religious phenomenon emerges when the desire to become one with the unconditional import of meaning detaches itself from the other element of religion, the affirmation of form. This happens when, on the soil of the basic sacramental attitude, the inner-religious dialectic has led to a destruction of particular sacramental forms and the theocratic will is lacking to actualize the unconditioned form. Mysticism is the radical ecstasy that seeks to grasp the import itself beyond all forms. In ecstasy, in the going beyond all forms of consciousness, or in submersion or absorption, in the sinking back into the ground of consciousness, mysticism finds its fulfillment. Mysticism is therefore like the undifferentiated sacramental spiritual situation, indifferent to conditioned forms. It does not participate in the theocratic struggle, even though it agrees in many ways with theocratic criticism. Consequently, it gives room to the demonic, and its own goal—the abolition of all forms, even of personality—is to be appraised as demonic as well as divine. Mysticism deliberately remains attached to the sacramental attitude. It does not want anything other than to grasp purely the import intended in the sacramental. It directs no criticism at myth and cultus; rather, it rises above both. Since, however, the apprehension of pure import without forms is impossible, even the radical mystic depends upon forms. He not only stands beyond the sacramental symbols but also uses them and gives them an ultimate deepening. Mysticism, then, is not a position of its own but rather the radical, critically conscious form of the sacramental attitude. Both are directed toward the Unconditional as present—sacramentalism in given, concrete forms, mysticism beyond all form.

In contrast to all this, theocracy is directed toward the demanded Unconditional, toward pure form. It is the reformatory movement in the historical development of religion. While the sacramental tendency provides the main stem and the enduring basis of the religious life, the theocratic tendency manifests itself in great reform movements: for example, in Jewish prophecy, primitive Christianity, Mohammedanism, Christian sects, Protestantism, and especially Calvinism. In all these instances the antidemonic struggle is taken up, and the demand is raised for a just social order, an ethical form of personality, a true knowledge of God. Immediate union with the Unconditional through participation in sacramental things and practices is rejected. Fellowship with the holy import takes place through validity of form. Purity in the ethical sense is a prerequisite for participation in the Holy. The divine is the infinite demand. But if theocracy were to affirm in the law only its form, it would cease to be religion and would become autonomous ethics or metaphysics. So long as it is still religion, it knows the God who is present even in the law, but his holiness is manifest in the unconditional demand. From this there arises in the perfected ethical theocracy the enormous tension between the unconditional demand and the conditioned, demonically dominated reality. This tension gives rise on the one hand to the phenomena of religious despair and on the other to the breakthrough to the religion of grace as a synthesis of theocratic and sacramental tendencies. The theocratic-reformatory principle is therefore the decisively moving element in the history of religion. From it come both the dissolution of sacramentalism and the breakthrough to the synthesis of the religion of grace. On the other hand, the sacramental spiritual situation, even in its mystical dissolution, provides the enduring basis from which all movements proceed, which can never be wholly abandoned, and to which all movements return in paradoxical synthesis.

The theocratic movement, however, is not simply the bearer of the inner-religious development. Upon it also depends the possibility of autonomous culture. For theocracy and autonomy have this in common, that they are directed toward form. They are to be distinguished only in the fact that theocracy seeks form as the bearer of unconditioned import whereas autonomy seeks it for its own sake.

b. The History of Religion and the Normative Concept of Religion

From these presuppositions the main tendencies of religious history can be presented as follows: the sacramental spiritual situation as the point of departure of all movements is indifferent to the distinction between the divine and the demonic. This stage has been characterized as the religion of nature. But this concept is misleading, for nowhere is nature worshiped as such. Nature provides the symbols, but what they signify is not nature. It is much more accurate to speak of a religion of indifference, keeping in mind, however, that in fact a pure indifference does not exist.

Against this sacramental lack of differentiation theocratic criticism arises, which can go so far as to bring about the autonomous expulsion of every sacramental import. But in its perfected religious form it must be characterized as a religion of infinite demand, a religion of law. Under the criticism of the religion of law sacramental religion can firmly cling to certain definite symbols and become heteronomous, *i.e.,* it can take up into itself the element of law. If, however, its concrete symbols are dissolved, it can be pushed forward into a *radical mysticism*. Insofar as mysticism aspires to go beyond everything given, it is also law, even though it be a law with the demand to abolish all law and all form within the conditioned order. It is possible, therefore, to sum up this whole situation created by theocratic criticism as the stage of law in religious development, in contrast to the previous stage of the immediately given sacramental attitude. The goal of the whole movement, however, is the union of the theocratic demand and mystical negativity with the sacramental sanctification of some *one* concrete thing. Now, since this unity of the present Holy and the demanded Holy cannot be deliberately brought about, but rather can be experienced only as a breakthrough, we describe it as "a religion of grace" *or* "a religion of paradox."

The synthesis of grace or of paradox is somehow actualized in every religion. It is actualized all the more purely and significantly, the more radical the theocratic element is, and the more difficult it thereby becomes for a relapse of the paradox into sacramental indifferentiation to take place. Where the theocratic spirit has not taken root, but where the sacramental attitude is destroyed, the result is the negation of every concrete presence of the Holy, i.e., the result is radical mysticism. But while grace can live in its paradox, mysticism must shatter in face of the contradiction of wishing to realize a form of consciousness in which consciousness together with all its forms is done away with. Yet mysticism, even in its radical form, is not without significance for the religion of paradox. In religious history it is the great, decisive criticism of empty, theocratic legalism, both autonomous and heteronomous. It is the most powerful symbol for directedness toward the holy import, and as such it is also the permanent background of the religion of paradox.

The above description of the basic tendencies of religious history and their normative synthesis is meant to provide the conceptual medium for the "construction" of the history of religion. The meaning of this construction does not lie in its schematic application to the particular religions. In reality, no tendency is to be found in an absolutely pure form. Every religion has elements of all tendencies in it; but the strength and kind vary in every instance and bring about the great varieties of religious history.

The attempt to set up a concept of religious norm as the synthesis of the different tendencies stands in contrast to two interpretations. One of these, in accord with the method of typological theory, views the tendencies alongside each other and as possessing equal value, while the other interpretation sees the ideal in a universal religion that includes all tendencies within itself in similar degree. Both are to be rejected. The typological interpretation does not at all belong to normative cultural science, whose nature it is to create concepts of norm. The opposite interpretation, however, leads to the ideal of a complex religion in which the different elements are not synthetically united but rather are brought together in merely external organization, i.e., legalistically.

These general definitions concerning the construction of the history of religion and concerning the concept of a religious norm are decisive for the concept of God and the concept of faith. The undifferentiated sacramental attitude symbolizes the Holy in manifold forms that have not found their synthesis in the unconditioned form, and therefore bear at the same time a divine and a demonic character. The nearer a religion stands to the undifferentiated attitude, the less it achieves authentic representations of God. Things in their immediate appearance are bearers of the

Holy. The stronger the form establishes itself, the more concept and intuition separate from each other, and the more a genuine polytheism is the result, whose highest form is a monarchical polytheism, as for example in the manner of Greek mythology. Through the dissolution of polytheism, mystical monotheism arises. It elevates itself beyond all particular divinities, and symbolizes the pure import in paradoxical concepts, like Nirvana, the Beyond, and the Abyss. But this mystical monotheism retains within itself the polytheism from which it was abstracted, precisely as the mystical attitude remains bound to the sacramental. Consequently, mystical monotheism can allow polytheism to persist or it can even completely fall back into it. A special manifestation of the sacramental concept of God is mythical dualism, as represented especially by the Persian religion and by the religions deriving therefrom. Here theocratic criticism has led to a concentration of the divine on one side and the demonic on the other. Dualism is to a high degree antidemonic; but at the same time it is itself subjected to the demonic, for it splits the absolute unity of form into two independent unities of form. Yet, the demonic is no unity of form, it is rather a form-bursting principle.

Pure theocracy is exclusively monotheistic. It negates the many divinities from the point of view of one God who is the bearer of the unconditioned form, the jealous God who tolerates no demonic cleavages. But the more God is removed from his polytheistic basis, the more abstract, transcendent and formal he becomes. The perfected religion of grace passes through the stage of exclusive monotheism. It does not remain, however, in this sphere of law, but rather takes from sacramental polytheism a symbol that brings to full expression the religious paradox: the symbol of the divine mediator. The finite, the conditioned, which in a paradoxical way is the bearer of the Unconditional and for whose sake it surrenders itself as a finite, the vision of the figure of the incarnate, lowly and dying God: this constitutes the genuine religious *mysterium*. Scarcely any religion is entirely without it; it is placed at the center of the mystery religions and in Christianity is raised to a status decisive for the history of religion. Naturally, the symbol as such is not decisive for the majesty and power of a religion. Only where the radical theocratic criticism has overcome every demonic element in the divine mediator and made him into a bearer of the unconditioned form, is the synthesis of the tendencies of the history of religions achieved. Only there can exclusive monotheism incorporate a polytheistic element without danger of demonic splitting, and thus be transformed from the religion of law to the religion of grace. The elucidation of this symbol in concrete form is the central task of the normative theory of religion, or theology.

The same polarities and syntheses hold also for the concept of faith. In the undifferentiated sacramental situation faith is not distinguished from autonomous "unfaith." The apprehension of all things is belief-ful, for they are all mediators of the Unconditional. Under the influence of the criticism of form an element of unbelief, which at the same time is autonomous obedience to form, penetrates into the faith and characterizes a large number of forms of faith as superstition. Superstition is a faith forced into the demonic by theocracy and by autonomous form. In mysticism faith is dissolved. It is replaced by a unification with the unconditioned import that far surpasses faith. The particular forms of things do not become objects of faith in a paradoxical way, but rather they are disregarded. Nevertheless, the mystical attitude is also belief-ful. It cannot dissolve the ultimate form, namely, being and consciousness; it can only break through. In radical theocracy the tension arises between unfaith in face of all finite forms and faith in the unconditioned form. A struggle of faith develops which ends either in a compromise between faith and unfaith or in faith in the paradox. Faith in the paradox, which in recognition of the unconditioned demand affirms the presence of the unconditioned import in a conditioned form, is the solution of the inner antinomy of faith.

It is not the task of philosophy of religion to decide what concrete symbol the religion of paradox can adopt, or better, what concrete symbol is fundamental for the normative concept of religion. That is the task of theology, which is necessarily confessional because it involves acknowledgment of a concrete symbol. But it does not therefore need to be less universally valid than philosophy of religion. If it has grasped the paradoxical, symbolic character of the content of faith, it must also place itself and its apprehension of the Unconditional under the No of the Unconditional. It will stand all the deeper in the religion of paradox, the more it succeeds in intuiting in its own symbol the No of the Unconditional against every symbol.

c. The Religious Tendencies in Autonomous Culture

The analysis of meaning has shown that culture in substance is religious, even though it is not so by intention. It must consequently be possible to encounter also in culture the same basic tendencies that we have observed in the inner-religious development. The difference is only this, that culture, because it is directed to the particular forms and their law, does not carry in itself the negativity of the Unconditional against every form. Accordingly, religious ecstasy disappears and with it the ecstatic, symbolic character of religious objects; in its place emerge enthusiasm and the subjectively creative quality that characterizes culture. There is certainly an ecstatic, form-bursting element in enthusiasm and in creativity. But it does not reach out beyond the form, and it dare not allow even the perfected form to disappear in the abyss of the Unconditional. The word "enthusiasm" (imbued with the divine) originates in the religious sphere. It has increasingly detached itself, however, from its basically religious meaning, and serves as a useful concept for the distinction between the religious and the cultural attitude.

In spite of this difference the opposition between the various tendencies we have observed in religion is also at work in culture. There can of course be no analogy in culture for the first of these tendencies, sacramental indifference. For it is precisely characteristic of the undifferentiated spiritual situation that a specifically holy form has not yet been indentified within it. But neither can there be a cultural analogy for the religion of paradox, for it is essential to it that a concrete form be the bearer of the unconditioned import. The religion of paradox thereby stands beyond the cultural sphere and represents a synthesis of the cultural and the religious. Only the opposition between the sacramental and the theocratic, an opposition that appears in the religious sphere after it has undergone the criticism of form, can become clearly evident in culture.

In analogy with the sacramental tendency in religion, culture creates the basic attitude of pantheism. In analogy with the theocratic tendency it creates critical rationalism. Just as religious history oscillates in the polarity between the sacramental and the theocratic, so cultural history, viewed in its ultimate intention, moves back and forth in the opposition between pantheism and critical rationalism. The question concerning the religious character of both tendencies is accordingly to be answered in this way: it is by no means permissible to assign one of these two forms—say pantheism—to religious history and to exclude the other from it.

Critical rationalism, just like pantheism, is directed toward the absolute synthesis, that is to say, as demand. And pantheism is just as little directed toward the Unconditional as such as is ethical rationalism, for as little as the latter is it aware of the negativity of the Unconditional, the negativity directed against even the perfected synthesis of forms. Pantheism is no more religious than ethical rationalism. Both, however, live from religion. Yet there is a difference between the two insofar as autonomous culture as a whole stands on the ground of the theocratic criticism of form, and thus stands with theocratic criticism in common opposition to sacramentalism. Now when within culture the opposition between the sacramental and the theocratic appears as an opposition between pantheism and critical rationalism, the resultant cultural attitude is that of critical rationalism, for within it the infinite striving for form, the root of cultural autonomy, becomes clearly evident. Pantheism, on the other hand, the affirmation of the world as a perfected unity of meaning, gives to things a kind of sacramental consecration. It does this not in the mode of sacramental indifference (for pantheism has undergone the criticism of form), but yet in such a way that the infinite demonic contradiction of the unity of form is overlooked and the unconditioned abyss of meaning is forgotten. Pantheism is idealism. As idealism, however, it shatters on the reality of the demonic, and is naturally replaced by a pessimistic-demonic *Weltanschauung*. Pantheism is viable only so long as it is supported by the import of mystical monotheism. The more this import recedes—and it must recede as a result of the tendency toward form—the more idealistic and unreal pantheism becomes.

But critical rationalism is also not viable on its own. Out of concern for the infinite demand that can never become a reality it loses the sacramental import that lives in genuine theocracy. Its place is taken by the demonic in naturalistic form; it breaks culture apart, and after a period of anarchy it strives to establish new sacramental bonds. The tragedy of autonomous form in Greek cultural history is the great, unmatched example in the history of religion for the outcome of radical autonomy. Just as pantheism lives from the sacramental, so critical rationalism lives from the theocratic, and both disintegrate when they have fully forsaken these their foundations.

Autonomous culture, moreover, is destined to pass over into the religion of paradox. Through the concrete symbol culture is freed alike from the infinity of criticism that ends in emptiness and also from the unreality of an idealistic perfection. In the concrete symbol the immediate presence of the Unconditional is intuited and experienced, and the antidemonic struggle is concretely represented and actualized. Conversely, autonomy of culture is the decisive safeguard against the regression of the religion of grace to heteronomous sacramentalism. In both tendencies, in the sacramental as well as in the theocratic, autonomy provides this safeguard. The pantheistic tendency prevents the concrete symbol from producing a heteronomous constriction of interest. It effects a radiation of the sacramental from the central symbol to all reality. It creates a pansacramentalism that is tied to form and nevertheless does not remain idealistic but finds the realistic ground of its faith in the concrete symbol. The critical-rationalistic motive, on the other hand, prevents the influence of the theocratic formative power from being limited to an inner religious circle, and causes it instead to assume the task of subjecting reality in all spheres to rational form. Yet in this task it is supported by a concrete, meaning-giving symbol and as a result is not swallowed up by the emptiness of infinite, rational criticism.

Thus all the essential elements of religion and culture join together in the religion of paradox, and they create the theonomous spiritual situation that is the goal of all realization of meaning, a goal inherent in the very nature of meaning itself.

PART TWO § THE CATEGORIES OF RELIGION

—— §§§ ——

1. The Religious Categories of the Theoretical Sphere

a. MYTH

A decisive result of the theory of the essence of religion was the insight that religion is not one function alongside others but the turning of the spirit toward the Unconditional, a directedness that supports all the functions. A philosophical theory of the categories of religion must accordingly concern itself with the appearance of the religious element in the individual spheres of meaning. It must show which categories are constitutive for religious objects in the various spheres, how these categories change in face of the tendencies within the history of religion, how they are related to the secular-cultural categories, and how they come into a normative context through the normative concept of religion. In contrast to the first part of the philosophy of religion, which treats the essence of religion as equally operative in all areas of meaning and which consequently could also be called the general theory of the categories of religion, we are now concerned with the special theory of categories which could also be characterized as a philosophical theory of phenomena. The special theory of the categories of religion is divided, in terms of the structure of the functions of meaning, into a theoretical and a practical part. The first concerns the categories of religious metaphysics, the second the categories of the religious ethos; for metaphysics is a theoretical, and ethos a practical, directedness toward the Unconditional.

In the theoretical sphere we distinguish between the philosophy of myth and the philosophy of revelation. Revelation is the form in which the religious object is given theoretically to religious faith. Myth is the form of expression for the content of revelation.

In *myth* the logical and the aesthetic apprehension of the Unconditional come together. The myth is not only aesthetic: it aims to give expression to the true and the real. And it is not only logical: it aims to apprehend intuitively the import of the Unconditional. The two are united in the original myth.

The nearer a religion stands to sacramental indifference, the more the intuition of everything has a mythical character, so that one is hesitant to speak of myth in connection with this spiritual situation generally. Indeed, for precisely that reason one does not, strictly speaking, find myth here, because everything real has immediate mythical qualities, because all of these immediately mythical realities, though later on to be secularized, are still sufficiently powerful symbolically to be an expression of the Holy, and finally because the opposition of holy and profane has not yet attained an essential significance. Only when the secularizing effect of theocratic criticism and autonomous form is evident, only when conceptualization subordinates the individual to the universal and devaluates it, and when the spiritual personality frees itself from mystical bondage to nature, does the myth take on more concrete forms. The Holy is concentrated upon over-arching figures (*Gestalten*) conceived as personal, that is, the gods, while holy men and things are reduced either to a divinely-hostile demonic estate or to mediators of revelation, and thus to bearers of a mediated holiness. This is the mythology of the great culture religions in which a sphere of highest holiness (the world of the gods, usually with a monarch at the head), stands above a sphere of lower spirits and demons. This sphere in turn serves as a transition downward to hierarchically graded forms of holiness in the personal and material sphere.

Against this polytheistic mythology there emerge on the one hand an inner-religious process of disintegration which leads to the mystical emptying of the myth, and on the other hand theocratic criticism which tries to abolish the myth altogether. Both can make use of the monarchical tendencies of the myth. Mysticism does not really negate the myth, but rather empties it through its abstract symbols. For that reason it can associate itself with the myth (especially with the hierarchical, graduated form of it) and can present itself as the highest level of the ladder, as for example in Neoplatonism. On the other hand, theocracy combats the myth with such force that it rejects even the name of its own symbols. It views the mythical—which is a universal category of the religious as such—as a special attribute of the demonically sacramental. But even then it cannot get along without the mythical symbols so long as it is religion and not a mere proclamation of law, that is, so long as it speaks of God and his action. With particular emphasis theocracy fights against the lower spheres of the Holy, against half-gods and demons, and against holy persons and things. Where it nevertheless takes over such concepts, it divests them of their mythical, sacramental holiness; they become functionaries in the theocratic shaping of the world. Their holiness is their obedience to pure form. Substantial holiness, however, is attributed to no finite thing.

In the religion of paradox the mythical element is again accepted, [only now] on the ground of the antimythical theocratic criticism. The intuition of an inner-divine tension and vitality overcomes the abstract legalistic character that God receives in pure theocracy. The religion of paradox struggles for a myth in which all demonic-mythical elements are eliminated and the unconditioned unity of the divine finds complete expression.

In autonomous culture the myth passes over into metaphysics. The formative powers of reason take possession of the holy symbols, now more in an aesthetic form, now more in a logical, and transform them into cultural creations. Metaphysics is alive so long as the holy import still inheres in its creations, so long as the sacramental element is preserved. Great metaphysics is full of mythical power, even though it is by intention directed no longer to the import, but rather to the form. But by reason of this formal intention its import is more and more lost, until rational science and art take its place. The criticism of rational metaphysics is the crisis in which it becomes evident that it is impossible to express the directedness toward the Unconditional through form alone. The metaphysics that is no longer a genuine myth, but also not a genuine science or art, shatters in face of rational criticism. And yet it is not possible to return to the myth that has been lost. The rational forms in science and art are too well established for that. But the more they have detached themselves from the unity expressed in the myth, the more they have been thrown into the empty infinity of the mere invention of forms, and the less possible it is for the spirit to live in them. Hence, there arises the longing for a new myth in which the rational forms will become symbols of the unconditioned import, that is, a longing for a theonomous metaphysics.

In the formulation of religious dogmas we encounter the attempt to develop a theonomous metaphysics. The concept of "dogma," through historical and especially canonical development, has taken on a heteronomous character. Dogma is the central object of attack for autonomous culture. But this opposition does not reckon with the actual matter in hand. By virtue of the insight into the symbolic character of all myth and the possibility of incorporating the infinite autonomous invention of form into myth, the "will to dogma" can become free again. Dogmatics is a theory of theonomous metaphysics or of myth with autonomous symbols. It is a central synthetic task for every period.

Myth presents itself in a threefold tendency: as a myth of being, a myth of history, and a myth of the absolute idea, or in the language of myth itself, as creation, redemption, and fulfillment. In this triad both poles of all things real and their ideal unity are apprehended from the point of view of the Unconditional: the immediately existent on the one hand and the meaning-fulfilling spirit on the other, and finally the perfected unity of being and spirit. The absence of any one of these is a sign of declining mythical power. Only in their unity does the relation of the Unconditional to the conditioned come to complete expression, and only then is a true symbolism achieved.

b. Revelation

We speak of revelation wherever the unconditioned import of meaning breaks through the form of meaning. Faith is always based on revelation, for it is an apprehension of the unconditioned import through conditioned forms. Autonomous unbelief knows of no revelation, it knows only about the creation of forms. But behind every real creation stands revelation; for every creation lives from the import to which it gives form. Heteronomous faith does not see the breakthrough quality of revelation. It gives to the mediator of revelation the absoluteness of revelation itself and thereby destroys the autonomous creation of forms. The struggle between heteronomous interpretation and autonomous repudiation of revelation is only to be settled by insight into the paradoxical, symbolic character of revelation.

The undifferentiated sacramental attitude knows no difference between revelation and the creation of forms. Everything that has esctatic qualities—and there is scarcely anything that could not possess them—is a bearer of revelation. Everything real has the inner powerfulness and intrinsic significance to serve as a bearer of the unconditional import. Under the influence of the criticism of form things more and more lose their revelational quality. Revelation becomes a special activity of divine beings which comes about by means of a revelational miracle. In place of the ever-present manifestation of the divine appears the document of revelation which owes its origin to divine inspiration. The document of revelation wins decisive significance especially on strongly theocratic soil as an aftereffect of severe antidemonic struggles. It acquires the exclusiveness of theocratic monotheism and becomes a bearer of the revelational law. But faith longs for the immediate presence of the Holy. It takes the side of the spirit in opposition to the letter. But since it is now bound to the unconditioned authority of the revelational document, it creates a holy exegesis that aims to make present the import of revelation from the past, without negating the authority of revelation. Occasionally, to be sure, the bond with the past is broken, and an immediate revelational ecstasy appears which combats the letter and appeals to the inner word. But as soon as it disavows the theocratic struggle of the past (that is, the history of revelation), it sinks down into demonic subjectivism.

Mysticism rises above the sphere of particular revelations. It wants revelation in an absolute sense, a revelation that stands beyond all forms and every particular revelation. It also devaluates the records of revelation, but not in order to put its own revelations in their place; that is, it does not do this from the perspective of rational criticism but rather in order to find behind all particular revelations the eternal revelation itself.

The religion of paradox intuits in a concrete revelational symbol the unity of theocratic exclusiveness and sacramental immediacy. The most significant example of this is the Pauline doctrine of the Spirit. The Spirit is an immediately present bearer of revelation, it has all the characteristics of genuine revelation, the ecstatic, the miraculous, the inspirational. At the same time, however, it is bound to the theocratically exclusive symbol of the Christ. Through this connection it is prevented from becoming a spirit of "disorder" and from sinking into the subjectively demonic. Its two works are *Gnosis* and *Agape,* the creation of theonomous knowledge and of theonomous community. Form and import are radically fused together; the ideal synthesis of revelation is clearly expressed.

All inner-religious conceptions of revelation are one in the fact that revelation is the unconditioned import breaking through form. The more these conceptions limit revelation to certain exclusive bearers of revelation, the more they are in danger of heteronomously perverting the concept of revelation. Miracle becomes a special event of nature destroying the natural form, inspiration becomes a supernatural communication shattering the form of consciousness, and the whole of revelation becomes a form of its own which contradicts the autonomous unity of form and rules out the autonomous criticism and creation of form. Here is the point where autonomy raises its sharpest opposition to religious heteronomy. It rejects miracle as a supernatural event, that is as a form-shattering event, and likewise rejects inspiration as the supernatural presentation of information, which splits the unity of consciousness; and it rejects the whole of revelation as a setting up of a form of its own above autonomous forms. But autonomy goes a step further. It sets autonomous creativity in the place of a breaking through of the unconditioned import. Revelation is replaced by the rational invention of forms, and the anticipatory presence of the Unconditional by an activity that wants to create something unconditioned. But the Unconditional cannot be created. The attempt of autonomy to dissolve revelation into spiritually autonomous fulfillment through meaning, to dissolve the history of revelation into cultural history, destroys revelation but is thereby also self-destructive. For the spirit is creative only insofar as the import of revelation is at work in it.

The opposition between an autonomous and a heteronomous doctrine of revelation is overcome by insight into the character of revelation as the manifestation of import breaking through form. Miracle is the ecstatic, symbolically powerful natural phenomenon, inspiration the ecstatic, symbolically powerful fulfillment of the spirit, the bearer of revelation the ecstatic, symbolically powerful personality. But ecstasy and symbolic power break through rather than shatter form. Rational autonomous criticism, even of the most holy bearers and documents of revelation, cannot be prevented by appeal to their revelational character. On the other hand, no criticism of the character of revelation can deprive a bearer of revelation of this quality, for it rests upon faith and symbolic power. Only the inner-religious, antidemonic criticism can destroy symbolic power and faith.

The paradoxical concept of revelation makes the intellectualistic misinterpretation of revelation impossible. Revelation is in no way a communication of objective information. This view is necessarily connected with the objectification of the concept of God, and is overcome by the insight into the symbolic character of all concepts that apprehend and interpret the Unconditional. The paradoxical concept of revelation opens the way for the theonomous faith issuing from revelation.

The question concerning the certainty of revelation is also answered thereby. In every act of revelational faith two things are involved: on the one hand directedness toward the unconditional import and on the other the symbolic form through which the Unconditional is revealed. Directedness toward the unconditional import has unconditional certainty; the certainty of faith is the absolutely fundamental certainty. Since this certainty is in no way directed toward an objective reality, it cannot be brought into doubt by means of the criticism of forms. On the contrary, it grounds the possibility of every certainty of form and of every criticism of form. The certainty of faith is consciously or unconsciously operative in every autonomous act, even in doubt; indeed, it usually is especially powerful there. It is quite different with the symbols in which revelation is intuited. They stand entirely under the criticism of form, and their certainty is the certainty of conviction that belongs to every creative, spiritual act. But it is the depth of religious certainty that it places even the certainty of its own symbols under the No, in order to avoid attributing the dignity of the Unconditional to any conditioned thing.

2. The Religious Categories of the Practical Sphere

a. The Cultus

Cultus is the sum total of those activities through which the Unconditional is to be realized in the practical sphere. All religious activity is cultic. Religious activity, however, is belief-ful activity. All belief-ful activity is therefore cultic. This general concept of cultus is able to do justice to all forms of religious activity, and provides the clear parallel to the form of belief-ful cognition, i.e., to myth.

The relation of myth and cultus is such that every cultic act has a mythical content, and every mythical object has a cultic realization. This complementarity of the two is based upon the faith character of both functions. For faith there can be no practical act that would not be directed toward the Unconditional through and beyond a symbol. And for faith there can be no symbol of the Unconditional toward which no practical act is directed. The act without symbolic content remains caught within the subjectivity of feeling. The symbol without a practical act remains in the objectivity of things. In neither case is there yet an attitude of faith, i.e., a presence of the Unconditional, a presence that breaks through all form. The one is an unbelief-ful subjectivizing, the other an unbelief-ful objectivizing, of the Holy.

In the indifferently sacramental spiritual situation the cultic act is undifferentiated from the secular act. Every active relation to things and men has sacramental qualities, and is supported by the presence of the Holy. Since all things possess a symbolic character, the relation to them is belief-ful even if the things in question are things of technical use. The goal of belief-ful activity is union with the holy ground of things, whether it be in dedication or in appropriation, in giving or in receiving. In this way the actions of daily life in nature and in community and also in inner psychic acts acquire a sacred significance. The secular and holy purposes are not yet differentiated. It is, therefore, not as if the Holy were put in the service of secular purposes, as rationalistic psychology supposes. Rather, the secular as secular has not yet appeared. Daily actions have a cultic religious quality in unity with their utility value. The latter is not the primary element, with the former something added to it and derived from it; rather, both are originally one. Naturally, the possibility exists of an unbelief-ful manipulation of the Holy; but it is not the essence of the original cultus, only its distortion.

The two fundamental acts of the cultus, the union with the Holy in dedication and in appropriation, come together in the act of sacrifice, the central cultic symbol. Sacrifice is the dedication of the conditioned to the Unconditional. A presupposition of union with the Unconditional is self-renunciation of the conditioned, the sublation of conditioned forms and of conditioned relations. Where this happens it makes possible the becoming imbued with the powers of the Unconditional which prove to be at work even in the conditioned relationships: blessing rests upon sacrifice. Even here one encounters the rationalistic misinterpretation of sacrifice, and it makes the misuse into a norm. It interprets sacrifice as a rational bargain in accord with the formula: *do ut des*. But genuine sacrifice is a union with the Unconditional that is present in everything real. The Holy is always at the same time that which is destructive and demanding of sacrifice and that which is fulfilling and life-bestowing.

The union of the sacrificer with the Holy depends upon the presence of the Holy in the object of sacrifice and upon its communicating itself to him. This happens with a special intuitive power in the sacrificial meal which signifies an immediate reception of the sacramental powers. The more in later polytheism the complex of social ideas is absorbed into the cultus, the more the sacrificial gift and the recipient of the sacrifice become separated from each other. In the religion of grace the original meaning of sacrifice is again taken up in a paradoxical way.

Sacrifice by nature has an ecstatic character that breaks through the secular concern for utility. The ecstatic attitude of mind of the sacrificer corresponds to this. In every cultus, ecstatic states that break through the consciousness are striven for and achieved through a holy means of transport. The naturally secular, form-bound consciousness cannot receive the Holy. All things connected with the cultus express this ecstatic character, the holy word, the holy song, the sacred vestments, the sacred place, etc.

A prerequisite for participation in the cultus is purity, that is, the renunciation of all qualities that obstruct ecstasy. From this arise the rites of purification preparatory to the cultus, through the completion of which a union with the Holy is alone possible.

The more the cultus is bound up with definite cultic myths, sacrificial forms and rites of purification, the more impossible it is for all and sundry individuals to perform the cultic act rightly. A separate, cultically pure caste emerges which at the same time possesses the knowledge of the cultus and performs the cultic functions for others—the priesthood.

With the increasing personalization and transcendence of the Holy in the polytheistic culture religions, the personal and the social categories in the cultus gain predominance. The union with the Holy becomes a personal relation to God, sacrifice becomes personal devotion, ecstasy becomes a state of being imbued with the concrete God. God as the bearer of forms becomes Lord and Ruler, the cultus becomes divine service (*Gottesdienst*). The ecstatic word becomes personal prayer. The old sacrifices and rites of purification lose their immediately sacramental character and become acts of devotion. In pure theocracy they lose their significance altogether. In their place appears the realization of the pure form: obedience is better than sacrifice. Divine service is the establishment of the sovereignty of God, sacrifice is the renunciation of one's own will. The priest becomes the teacher of the Law. Purity is a moral quality. Ecstasy is suppressed, and the demonry of transport is overcome. The cultus has in principle passed over into ethos. Of course, this does not actually happen within the religious sphere; the personal relation to God remains. Prayer acquires decisive significance. It becomes the plea for a pure heart, that is, for fulfillment through the qualities of moral holiness. This prayer is interpreted at the same time as the perfect sacrifice, because in it dedication of the will is accomplished. Even here we still find cultus and all its characteristics. Within religion, cultus can no more be dissolved than myth. But it is a cultus that, in its abstract unconditionedness, must either lead to despair of any union with the holy God or move into the secular dissolution of the cultus, unless it breaks through this tension to the religion of paradox.

Pure mysticism penetrates and identifies the symbolic character of cultus and goes beyond it through an ecstasy that no longer employs concrete forms. Rather, it rises above every sacrificial form, rite of purification, and priesthood, and achieves cultic union in the absolute sacrifice of all forms of reality. But this ecstasy also requires preparation, indeed the whole life is a process of purification. Mystical *askesis* is the absolute form of the cultic idea of purification, and from this point of view the other cultic forms are ranked in value. The cultus is not criticized but transcended.

113

The religion of paradox breaks out of the indissoluble tension into which radical theocracy has driven the cultus. The cultus has reality only insofar as it is supported by the "gracious" presence of the Unconditional. The presupposition of the cultus is grace. Grace is the correlate of revelation in the practical sphere. It is the presence of the Unconditional in conditioned forms, apprehended through action. It is the divine activity to which human activity responds. In the sacramental spiritual situation grace is identical with fullness of life in general. In polytheism it is focused upon definite acts of divine giving and helping. In theocratic criticism it is identical with the gift of the Law. But just by that fact it is as grace sublated and transformed into pure demand. Like myth and revelation, cultus and grace approach the boundary of their self-dissolution within radical theocracy. But dissolution does not really take place; instead, we find the tension between form and import, between demand and gift, which leads to the breakthrough of the religion of paradox, of the true religion of grace. The cultus in the religion of paradox unites the two elements in which the sacramental and the theocratic cultus culminate, prayer and sacrifice. Prayer, however, is not primarily prayer for a pure heart but rather for forgiveness of sins, that is, for that form of grace which is given immediately with the theocratic relation to the Unconditional. Under the aegis of the paradoxical concept of "justification by faith" this form of grace becomes the center of the Pauline and Protestant doctrine of grace. Simultaneously, however, the presence of God is intuited in sacramental fashion in the concrete symbol of the divine, self-sacrificing mediator; to participate in his self-dedication is redemption and fulfillment. And both elements, the theocratic and the sacramental, are one. The divine sacrifice is the forgiveness of sins, and vice versa. The grace of God is the divine sacrifice. In this way a cultus is made possible into which all forms of the original cultus can enter, though purified through antidemonic criticism and perceived in their symbolic character. The cultic is nothing other than the most highly concentrated form of belief-ful activity. But all activity ought in essence to be belief-ful activity. The union with the Unconditional, the apprehension of its gracious presence, which is ecstatic fulfillment in sacramentalism and personal obedience in theocracy, becomes in the religion of paradox *spiritual love,* the synthesis of ecstasy and obedience.

In autonomous culture belief-ful activity is replaced by unbelief-ful activity bound to form. Autonomous ethos takes the place of cultus. And ethos is directedness toward the Unconditional in the realm of action. Autonomous ethos, therefore, carries within itself the contradiction that it aims to realize the Unconditional through conditioned forms. It is thus similar to autonomous metaphysics, which wishes to do the same thing in the theoretical sphere. And just as autonomous metaphysics lacks revelation, so autonomous ethos lacks grace. And like the former, it collapses by reason of its inner contradiction and breaks down into the two spheres that are united in cultus, i.e., the personal function (oriented to law) and the social function. The relationship of personality to things is no longer determined by the concern for cultic union but rather by the subjugation of the thing to law and by its rational utility. Social relations are determined by formal justice, which appears in place of cultic righteousness and purity. In the social sphere directedness toward the unconditional Love is replaced by the ethos of the cultivated personality and the community that promotes culture. In place of cultic ecstacy we now find "culture" (*Bildung*) and form. Of course, it is also true here that so long as the autonomous ethos still bears a living power, it unconsciously retains a quality of grace and a cultic character. In the demand for righteousness we see an enthusiasm oriented to the future, in the idea of the spiritually disciplined personality and community we see enthusiasm oriented to intuition.

Here, too, in the autonomous ethos we find the opposition between the sacramental and the theocratic. But, as everywhere in culture, the theocratic attitude oriented to form is the more consistent of the two. As a critical rationalism it reveals the unreal, idealistic character of any pantheistic, intuitive ethos. It itself, however, leads to the emptiness of pure autonomous form, a condition that is inadequate in the practical as well as in the theoretical sphere, and thus it has to drive on toward a theonomous ethos.

In the autonomous sphere the central act that takes the place of sacrifice is unbiased dedication to form. The more unconsciously cultic it is, the more it is real sacrifice, and the more it bears a real fulfillment. But the more unbelief-ful, empty and formal it is, the more it becomes a loss without a gain. This can also be seen from the point of view of the object: the richer and more creative the forms are, all the more is the import present in them, all the more are they the bearers of grace, and all the more can they be a source of cultic experience. The more empty the forms have become, the more secular and meaningless is their effect; no *communio* is possible with this rationally abstract world, this graceless law.

In autonomy the *bearer of the creation of form, the shaper,* the seer, and the leader, takes the place of the priesthood, in the theoretical as well as in the practical sphere. Devotion becomes æsthetic intuition of the forms of reality, prayer becomes the integration and exaltation of the personal life. But in all these relations the same things hold which we have said in general about autonomy: the sacramental intuitive attitude is idealism, and critical rationalism reveals the emptiness of mere form, and under the impact of severe social-ethical shocks, forces a turning toward theonomous ethos.

The union of ethos with cultus in theonomy, however, is of decisive significance not only for culture but also for religion. It prevents cultic activity from heteronomously "violating" and perverting cultural activity. It compels the recognition that all cultus is symbolic, that the special cultic forms are not forms in the proper sense but rather are representations of the living import inherent in all activity. This, however, does not mean that cultus as such is merely representational activity. Where cultus is so understood it is assigned to the aesthetic sphere and loses its essence. Cultus is a real activity, for all belief-ful activity, and that means all meaning-fulfilling activity in a theonomous spirit, is cultus. Only the special cultic forms are symbolic. Not their inherent value but their symbolic power is stronger than that of other activity. But even these cultic forms—prayer for the forgiveness of sins as well as devotional union with the God who gives himself graciously—stand like all activity and all cognition and everything real under the No of the Unconditional.

b. THE CULT FELLOWSHIP

The bearer of the cultus is the cult fellowship. Like everything spiritual, religion is supported by a community. The religious consciousness would remain without the element of unconditioned demand if in the community the law of what is right and moral did not acquire unconditional validity. And the presence of the Holy would not have the character of revelation and grace if the individual could at will establish it by works instead of having to participate in the Holy as it is presented in history and community. Therefore the individualism of religious feeling is as irreligious as is the naturalism of a religionless education or the rationalism of a new religion. Community and tradition are rooted in the character of the Holy as that which is valid and is a gift of grace. Even the mystical and monastic hermits live from the import of the community. In their lives they represent cultically and symbolically the community-negating element of this community.

In the sacramentally undifferentiated spiritual situation the cult fellowship is identical with the totality of sacramentally sacred communities of social and legal character. Family, race, nation, state, and locus with their different communal and power relations are bearers of the cultus. The individual has value only in terms of his significance in the context of the whole. He does not possess any cultic quality of his own.

Through theocratic criticism the sacred fellowship increasingly separates itself from its connection with the demonically permeated sacramental communities. The unconditional demand for righteousness and love is directed toward the individual and draws him apart into the "communion of the saints." In sacramentalism personal piety expresses itself as a power of ecstasy within the established forms; but in theocracy it becomes the supporting power of the sacred community. This gives rise to the *voluntary* fellowship and to religious personalism. A radical criticism is directed against the sacramental consecration of natural communities and sacramental-aristocratic personalities. All sacred immediacies, from the love of the child to the bonds of national community, must break down before the unconditioned demand. The sacred community transcends all particular communities. Thus the missionary world-churches come into existence. The more radically theocratic these movements are, the more they attempt, in the light of the sacred demand, to regulate all forms of public and private life and of state and law, and to extirpate the irrational demonic powers. This explains the rise of powerful eschatological movements that aim to prepare for the coming kingdom of God and like all radical theocracy either break through to the religion of grace or end in compromise. The most remarkable example of this is English Puritanism.

The mystic isolates himself from all community, nevertheless without criticizing it. He shatters the traditional forms of personality and thus also of community, and in absolute ecstasy he stands forth as "the alone with the alone" (Plotinus). And yet even he draws the strength of his life from the sacramental import of the cult community and from the mystical traditions that cultically elevate him to the absolute cultic act, namely, self-dissolution.

In the religion of paradox the cult fellowship is not identical with the immediately given communities, nor does it stand over against these communities as a critically dissolving demand. Rather, from the point of view of its concrete symbol it gives to all immediate forms of community a paradoxical-sacramental consecration, that is, a consecration that has undergone theocratic criticism and which has internalized the critical, negative element for all aspects of life. The kingdom of God is not a pure form but rather the paradoxically present and yet ever demanded holy fellowship. The perfect realization of this synthesis is an ideal. In the historical religions the tension does not cease between the sacramental and the theocratic, a tension that comes to expression in the opposition between the sacramental *Volkskirchen* on the one hand and the theocratic sects and communal-movements on the other.

In autonomous culture the cult fellowship is replaced by the autonomous community of law and the secular association. The decisive thing is concern for form. Even here, however, much of the cultic quality is preserved (*aufgehoben*). Through every creative ac-

tivity in state and society, through every struggle for personal fulfillment, something of the directedness toward the unconditioned
community and unconditioned personality continues to pulsate.
Also the autonomous communities like the cult community, draw
their vitality from the grace in which they wish to participate and
through which alone they can be creative. Accordingly, we find
here also the two basic tendencies, the sacramental on the one
hand which gives an ethical sanctification to the ideally intuited,
given forms of community, and the theocratic on the other which
strives for the universal human community of law and fights for it
with enthusiasm. Here again the critical, rational tendency is more
consistent. It makes evident the impossibility of holding to a pantheistic social idealism. But it leads to the "pure" form of society and
personality whose emptiness in all areas of economics, law,
pedagogy, and social order forces a turn toward a religiously
sacramental meaning-fulfillment.

In the religion of paradox the autonomous forms of law, community, and personality are incorporated into the cult community.
They prevent the heteronomous petrification of the cult community and its forms in opposition to the other rational forms of
community. The struggle between church and state, canonical and
secular law, religious and humanistic communal life, cultic and
cultural personality, comes to an end as soon as the holy fellowship and the holy personality have grasped their own symbolic
character. Their forms are not forms in the proper sense and
therefore do not stand beside or above the other proper, that is,
autonomous forms. Rather, they are paradoxical, that is, they
express in particular symbolic forms the intention toward the Unconditional contained in all social and secular activity. The demand for theonomy is thereby fulfilled.

The fundamental problem of philosophy of religion is solved in terms of the basic principles of the religion of paradox outlined above, adumbrated first in their general features and then in specific reference to the theoretical and the practical spheres. We have set forth a philosophy of religion which in method and elaboration has incorporated within itself the autonomy of religion and culture and has also pointed the way to a theonomous synthesis. We have attempted to provide a theonomous philosophy of religion which overcomes the conflict between theology and philosophy of religion, and to which a theology can be joined as a concrete elaboration and fulfillment.

II

The Conquest of
the Concept of Religion
in the Philosophy of Religion *

The paradoxical formulation of our title stands in need of justification. "Paradoxical" can mean "ingenious," but in that case the paradox is based upon an ambiguous and contradictory verbal formulation, and belongs in the aesthetic realm. The word can also be understood dialectically. Then it refers to the tension of two patterns of thought which are contradictory, though in themselves consistent and necessary. In this sense the paradox belongs in the logical realm. In both cases the paradox is a function of the subject, either of the caprice of artistic imagination or of the necessity of logical structure in thought. But there is a point where paradox is grounded completely in the object rather than in the subject, where paradox is as necessary to every assertion as consistency is to every empirical scientific assertion: the point at which the Unconditional becomes an Object. The fact that it becomes an object is indeed the primal paradox, since by its nature the Uncon-

* Translated by Kenneth Schedler with the assistance of Charles W. Fox.

ditional stands beyond the antithesis of subject and object. Thus, every statement about the Unconditional is necessarily in the form of paradox. Aesthetic and logical paradoxes are in principle resolvable. Both present a problem to be solved, either by common sense or by logical thought. But the paradox of the Unconditional is not resolvable. It poses a problem that calls for intuition (*Schauen*).

This appears to make philosophical statements regarding the Unconditional into religious ones. To this possibility it should be remarked that a philosophy of religion which stands apart from the religious reality is as absurd as an aesthetic unrelated to the actual world of art. In both cases one seeks to speak about an object whose sole given form remains inaccessible. But at the same time, reference to the thing itself can take on a quite contradictory form, if this contradiction arises solely out of the object itself. Thus Nietzsche, since he acted in the name of the God who spoke through him, had a right to fight against God; Strauss, on the other hand, had no such right, for it was the human, the all too human, that spoke through him. In this regard, it is on the basis of the religious reality itself that I indicate my spiritual affinity in the following ideas with men like Barth and Gogarten whose concern is the religious Word. I have been surprised to see how, without mutual influence, the unqualified affirmation of the Unconditional within philosophy of religion as in religious thinking proper has led us to the same position in principle. Nevertheless, the following lines of thought are to be understood in their own right; they are philosophical ideas and they aspire to be nothing other than philosophy. The paradoxical nature of every ultimate statement concerning the Unconditional does not compromise the rationality and necessity of the fundamental relationships out of which this paradox arises.

It remains to be demonstrated that the concept of religion contains within itself a paradox. "Religion" is the concept of a reality which through this very concept is destroyed. Yet the concept is unavoidable. The point is to use it in such a way that its destructive force is eliminated through its subordination to a higher concept. That, however, is the concept of the Unconditional. To be sure, the inner dialectic of the concept of religion makes a certain amount of ambiguity unavoidable, inasmuch as the concept is used, in a general orientational sense as well as in a more precise, polemical sense. This difficulty cannot be avoided, since every relatively new conceptual creation would fall into the same dialectic, and the meaning would have to be determined contextually.

Having established our basic problem, we will address it in four stages: (1) the protest of religion against the concept of religion; (2) the dominance of the concept of religion in philosophy of religion; (3) the conquest of the concept of religion; and (4) the dialectic of autonomy.

1. The Protest of Religion Against the Concept of Religion

There are four objections that religion raises against the concept of religion. First, it makes the certainty of God relative to the certainty of the self (*Ichgewissheit*). Secondly, it makes God relative to the world. Thirdly, it makes religion relative to culture. Fourthly, it makes revelation relative to the history of religion. In short, through the concept of religion the Unconditional is grounded upon the conditioned and becomes itself conditioned, and thereby destroyed.

a. The certainty of the Unconditional is unconditional. Nevertheless, whenever thinking is determined by the concept of religion, another certainty is believed to be more fundamental than that of the Unconditional, namely, the self's certainty of itself. The subject's self-certainty is given priority over the certainty of God. The self is seen capable of self-apprehension apart from any awareness of God. But self-certainty is no basis for unconditional certainty. When the objective world to which it is related dissolves into appearances, then self-certainty takes on the veil-like character of a dream. The subject falls with the object. On the other hand, the Unconditional stands beyond both subject and object. Only when the self is understood as the medium for the self-apprehension of the Unconditional, does it participate in unconditional certainty, whether this latter be expressed in terms of absolute life, as with Augustine, or in terms of absolute form, as with Descartes. But the Unconditional is always that which provides a ground, and the self is its medium and that which is grounded. Where this is not the case, and the self makes itself independent, religion, it is true, comes into being—but in losing God the self ultimately loses itself.

b. If the certainty of the Unconditional is lost, the Unconditional loses its reality as well. Religion remains as a function of the conditioned within the world of the conditioned, and it starts from this its own world in order to reach the Unconditional. Since religion has a self-sufficient conception of the world which needs only peripheral supplementation, God in this way becomes a correlate of the world but thereby himself part of the world. But the true Unconditional lies beyond both this God and the world. In this situation a God beneath God comes into being, namely, the God of deism. Or there is yet another alternative: namely, that the concept of the world needs no supplementation, that the universe is complete in itself, and God is identical with it. Here God is seen as the totality, the synthesis of all finite forms, identical with the universe of the conditioned (though this can never be the Unconditional). This God is the God of pantheism. Wherever the concept of the world is complete without God, God has become an empty name that one utters for the sake of religion, but which can be dispensed with completely, since it is all the same whether the universe is called "matter" or "spirit."

c. In effect the spirit of the concept of religion destroys not only the certainty and reality of God, but also religion itself. "Religion" is a function of the human spirit. It remains so, even when (along with Scholz) one makes it into a creation of God in man. For the human spirit must at least have the functional possibility for religion, and of course, nothing more than that is intended here. Consequently, religion stands alongside the other functions of the human spirit. But where? At first it sought haven in one of the other functions, namely, the practical. But autonomous ethics is complete in itself, and thus it either assimilates religion or drives it on to the theoretical function. But autonomous philosophy likewise has no need of religion, and so subordinates it to itself as a preliminary stage, as a transitional phase, assimilates it and drives it on to feeling. Feeling, however, accompanies every function, and therefore, one must always speak of a definite feeling, such as a feeling for the universe. But then if religion is identified with feeling, it is no longer the function but the object that determines religion. Thus, attempts are made to find the homeless one a place of its own: a province within the spiritual life (Schleiermacher), a religious *a priori* (Troeltsch), the highest category of act (Scheler). Just as a person is ethical, scientific, aesthetic, or political, so he is *also* religious. Here the Unconditional stands alongside the conditioned. But religion does not allow a person to be *also* religious; in fact, it does not grant that a person is "religious" at all. It tolerates no co-ordination of the functions, even the hierarchical form in which religion stands at the top. It is, rather, a consuming fire over against every autonomous function of the human spirit. He who would seek a religious *a priori* must be aware that all other *a priori's* thereby sink into the abyss. The concept of religion, however, knows nothing of this.

d. Just as the concept of religion dissolves the unconditionality of faith into the relativity of the various spiritual functions, so it also dissolves the unconditionality of revelation into the continuous evolution and alteration within the history of religion and culture. "Religion" as a general concept is indifferent to the revelatory claims of the particular religions. Absolute religion is a "square circle." Whenever Christianity has become religion, it *a priori* has lost its absoluteness. In this respect, Troeltsch's insistence upon the *a posteriori* was legitimate. At the most, faith gives the predicate "religion" to that religion which does not bring salvation, to false religion. "Religion" is a derogatory term, indicating that inferior quality within religion which consists in its failure to go beyond the subject. In that case it is nothing more than a God-ward intention that does not have God, because God has not manifested himself within it. And the content of this derogatory term then becomes the foundation upon which revelation is supposed to ground itself—and yet cannot. For if it does, revelation either becomes a transmission of knowledge which the autonomous spirit would have discovered anyway, and thereby deteriorates into a rationalism occasionally supplemented by the supernatural. Or it becomes cultural history (*Geistesgeschichte*) and is dissolved into the contingencies of the cultural process. If revelation is a "religious" concept, then it is no concept at all.

This is what is involved in the protest that religion raises against the spirit of the concept of religion. Let us see how this matter has been regarded up until now in the philosophy of religion.

2. The Dominance of the Concept of Religion in Philosophy of Religion

The development of philosophy of religion in the Western world has taken place in three periods (or typical forms): the rational, the critical, and the intuitive. Running concurrently with all three is the empirical philosophy of religion. The latter, however, can be left out of consideration, because it can be consistent only in its statements about the actualization of religion in the individual and historical life and not in those about religion itself. As soon as it tries to say something about religion itself, it borrows from one of the other methods.

a. In the rational period the dominance of the concept of religion is unconscious, in the critical period it is conscious, and in the phenomenological period it is declining. In the philosophy of the Renaissance, world-consciousness is still embedded in a mystical or ecstatic God-consciousness. Apart from God there is no world, just as, to be sure, in contrast to the Middle Ages, apart from the world there is no God. The distinction between nature and the supernatural is abolished. Nature is supernatural in quality, and the supernatural is nature itself. However, this was but a transition. Beginning with Galileo the mathematically-oriented natural sciences banished the supernatural. Nature becomes purely objective, rational, and technical; it becomes divested of the divine. It is now possible to have a concept of the world without having a concept of God. In this manner the way was made free for the dominance of the concept of religion. This becomes immediately evident at the beginning of the whole development, namely, in Descartes. The basis for certainty is the self, and God is inferred from the self. What is historically fateful here is not the fact that the principle of all rationality is found in the self's certainty of itself, for that principle certainly involves the unconditionality of logical form, which as unconditionality bears a quality of holiness within itself. But the real change in the total situation is to be seen in the contrast of the post-Cartesian outlook with, for example, that of Augustine. For no longer is the Unconditional element extracted out of self-certainty in order through it to apprehend God, but rather is the rational principle extracted, in order from it to deduce God. This becomes fully apparent for the first time in the philosophy of the Enlightenment, which sought, with the aid of the technical-objective category of cause and effect, to infer God from the world. The certainty of God is made to rest upon the certainty of the world and the power of logical inference. Here we see already the domination of the concept of religion, to be sure in concealed form, since in general God rather than religion remains the focus of discussion.

Kant correctly perceived that without an ontological proof this goal is unattainable. But the ontological way was no longer an open possibility. It is possible only where consciousness stands in immediate unity with the Unconditional. But then the ontological way is not a logical conclusion from the idea of the Unconditional to its existence (*Sein*), a procedure that, of course, is impossible. It is rather the expression of the unconditional certainty which the Unconditional has in face of everything conditioned insofar as the Unconditional stands beyond the antithesis of thought and being. As soon as consciousness of the world is rendered independent, and thinking and being are no longer connected, and God is objectified, this expression of a real (*realen*) state of consciousness becomes a syllogism whose premise is invalid. Thus, the critique of the ontological proof was the result of the spiritual development from the medieval to the modern period, from God-consciousness to autonomous world-consciousness. At the same time it marked the end of the rational period.

Corresponding to this concealed dissolution of the certainty of God is the concealed dissolution of his reality. Almost all the philosophers of this period have a world view in which God becomes the central element in the construction of the world. He is the bearer of world-harmony, the ingenious watchmaker of the cosmic system, the mediator between subject and object. Even when he is called the source of our ideas or that which is beyond thinking and extension, he is always understood in a technical and objectified manner, as though he were a thing. For through the deterministic idea of pre-established harmony, thinking has also become thingified (*dinghaft*). The God who is supposed to be a supplement to the world is not God but the world itself. Only Spinoza's religious depth overcomes these concepts unworthy of God and points toward the following period. But he, too, remained dominated by the contemporary thingified conception of the world, so that even in his view God becomes an absolute thing. He exposed the innate tendency of the concept of religion, and thus his contemporaries rightly saw in him the real danger of their time.

The unconditionality of religion over against culture was also abolished in a concealed manner. The *colere et intelligere Deum* stands alongside the *colere et intelligere* of man and the world. As God stands alongside the world, so also religion stands alongside science and politics, art and morality. Here, too, the destructive consequences of the concept of religion remain concealed. There is knowledge of the world—and *also* of God; there is the state—and *also* the church; there is art—and *also* cultus. Religion is still a universal phenomenon, but in all cases it is only one component and has lost its omnipresence. The same problem appears in the relation of the Unconditional to philosophy. The absoluteness of revealed truth emerges as the absoluteness of religion based on reason. Thus, revelation has become a chapter of metaphysics, and has been drawn into the dialectic of proof and refutation. As long as faith in absolute reason prevailed, in spite of all opposition, the consequences of the concept of religion remained concealed. When reason became historical, religion based on reason developed into the history of religion.

b. In the critical period the relativistic consequences of the concept of religion became apparent. The certainty of God loses its theoretical meaning. In terms of its true import the moral proof for the existence of God can do nothing more than endow moral autonomy with the sanctity of the Unconditional. But all the attempts of philosophical and theological Kantians to extract a theoretical existence of God from the Unconditional by means of ethical postulates are in vain. In this matter Neo-Kantianism had drawn the obvious conclusion from its critical foundation. The Philosophy of "As If" performed a distinct service for philosophy of religion in perceiving the fictional character of this theoretically existing God who was supposed to be provable through moral postulates. For the idealistic Kantians a certainty of God is not possible apart from certainty of the world. Religion is a special way of experiencing the world which either is sublated into philosophy, as in Hegel, or has an abiding unique significance, as in Schleiermacher. The effect of the concept of religion is most evident at the point where nominalistic thinking fails to recognize any objective conception of the world, as with Simmel, and religion is accordingly located exclusively in the subject. Religion becomes a rhythm or hue of the soul, an expression of its metaphysical significance, and thus a consecration not of the objective world, as in realism, but of the subjective life. The concept of religion, which sought to proceed from the self to God, has relapsed into the self.

Upon the horizon of the idea of God settle the threatening clouds of Spinozism from the preceding period, but it is a Spinozism stripped of its objectifying character by the (new) idealistic point of departure. No longer is God independent of the world. Deism becomes pantheism. God is the "world idea," the form of all forms, the ultimate synthesis, conceived either as a reality or as an infinite task. He is the world *sub specie aeternitatis*. In this manner the unity of God and the world is restored, but not, as in the Renaissance, from the side of God who has taken the world up into himself, but rather from the side of the world, into which God has been absorbed. Thereby the objective, scientific formation of concepts becomes here the pathway to God. The concept of the world is the creative basis for the concept of God and makes the latter dependent upon itself. This dependence upon the concept of the world is true not only for idealism, but also for subsequent developments. The concept of God follows the concept of the world along the paths of materialism, voluntarism, naturalism, and positivism. In so doing it reveals the impossibility of fulfilling the romantic yearning to reach God through the structure or form of the world, to reach a new immediacy, a new ontologically-oriented spiritual situation on the basis of the scientific apprehension of the world. Through its clear understanding of this situation it was again the Philosophy of "As If" which perceived that the concept of God had to lose its roots the moment God was degraded to the state of a derivative reality, instead of being recognized as the primordially given itself.

The results of all this also appear in the attitude of the critical period to our third point: in analogy with the transition from deism to pantheism, religion turns into culture. It is tacked on to one of the functions of the human spirit, and without fail is assimilated to this function. The effect of this transition upon the spiritual situation of the nineteenth century is clearly evident. Among individual Hegelian thinkers and among the working-class groups influenced by Hegel and Marx, science (*Wissenschaft*) usurps the role of religion; among the ethically-oriented middle-class, morality fills the gap left by religion; and among the most highly cultivated, the arts. The attempts to preserve religion as a special function fail, because its absoluteness brooks no relativization, and because the religious function called for here must revert into culture just as surely as the God prescribed by the deists reverts into world. Of course, it is not to be denied that culture in this way takes on a religious tone. But this quality comes to it as a supplement, and thus it can also be absent, and indeed is so as soon as the concept of the world comes to be seen in a materialistic or a voluntaristic rather than in an idealistic framework.

The victory of historical reason within idealism in this period signifies alike the victory of the history of religion. Throughout the period the latter was conceived as the history of revelation, naturally not in a supernatural sense, but in an immanent cultural-historical sense. It is God himself who comes to self-awareness within the finite in this history; it is the potencies of the world which become successively manifest in mythology and revelation. With the breakdown of the idealistic presupposition the history of revelation becomes a part of man's spiritual history whose meaning is absorbed into the general history of culture. Here, too, the concept of religion is completely victorious.

The critical period is more consistent than the rational period. Therein lies its superiority. It exposes the destructive consequences of the concept of religion, for religion itself, but it also achieves something positive. It represents a powerful reaction against the secularization and evisceration of the world which result from objectification. To be sure, this reaction remained romantic and aesthetic, and then reverted into its own opposite. For the destroyed religious consciousness cannot be restored through the will of individuals, but only through the fate of nations and masses. Nevertheless, the romantic philosophy of religion provides the bridges and creates the forms by means of which the new spirit of an ontological consciousness of God can again flow.

The world, culture and history all have qualities of holiness. They may have them, but they need not have them. But what if the order were reversed? What if we were to ask: must they have them? How would it be, if above all the religious dimension had the qualities of unconditionality and certainty, and the world, culture and history were tentative and dubious secularizations of the holy which needed to be overcome? With this question we turn our attention to the third, the intuitive period.

c. This third period begins at the turn of the century, not only in the form of phenomenological philosophy (in its narrower sense) but also in the general movement of spiritual life away from the objective-technical apprehension of the world to an immediate-intuitive one. It is more difficult to discuss this period, since it is still in process of development. Nevertheless, it is already possible to get a glimpse of its broadest contours. Its significance for the philosophy of religion lies in its conscious opposition to the dominance of the concept of religion. It seems prepared for a new ontologically-oriented spiritual situation. There are many manifestations of this tendency: Otto's apprehension of the numinous as a reality breaking through all objective forms, Scheler's elevation of the value of holiness above all other levels of value, and Scholz's complete separation of religious and theoretical existential judgments. We must now ask how successful these trends have been in exorcising the spirit of the concept of religion.

Both Scheler and Scholz seek vigorously to overcome the functional justification of religion: Scheler by ascribing primary certainty to the religious object rather than the religious act and thus by settling the God-question before considering the question of religion; Scholz by strongly opposing the interpretation of religion as an autonomous creation of the human spirit and seeing in the simple statement, "God is," the primary indication of the nature of religion. It could be argued that these views threaten to reinstate the rational method, but in reality this danger does not exist. God is not to be deduced from an established concept of the world by means of syllogisms, but rather his reality is to be directly intuited (*erschaut*) apart from any consideration of the world. In order to emphasize the difference of this intuitive perception (*Anschauen*) from objective-reflective knowledge of the world, Scheler builds up the apprehension of reality in stages: the scientific, metaphysical, and religious forms of knowledge. The way to overcome the rational as well as the critical method is without doubt thereby prepared. But it is still not attained, for it is not clear just how the levels are related to each other. The difficulties involved here become obvious when Scheler permits metaphysics to invalidate itself, by a *sacrificium intellectus,* for the sake of religion. Awareness of God is thereby made dependent upon a self-negating awareness of the world. The certainty of the world is sacrificed for the sake of the certainty of God; its reality is sacrificed for the sake of his reality. Yet the world makes this sacrifice. God lives on the basis of this sacrifice, and he disappears once the autonomous spirit refuses to make such a sacrifice. The autonomous spirit, however, must refuse this sacrifice in order to avoid the inner disruption occasioned by theoretical judgments coming from alien sources.

The Protestant philosopher of religion, Scholz, does not demand a *sacrificium intellectus,* but rather attempts to demonstrate to the intellect the credibility of religion. He thus presupposes a consciousness before which this credibility would have to be demonstrated. This consciousness is that of the moral personality. Confidence in the truth of a revelation can only be awakened by the ethical character of the bearer of revelation. Who could fail to see here the moral proof for the existence of God so deeply engrained in Protestantism, simply transposed into the personal key? In the case of both Scheler and Scholz, the certainty and reality of the world are retained as the basis for the certainty and reality of God. Scheler does so by making the world a stage, Scholz by making it a criterion. The only thing achieved is this duality: God is neither deduced from the world, as in the rational period, nor is he drawn into the world, as in the critical period.

As for our two other points, the relations of religion and culture, and revelation and history, Scheler again supports his views by appeal to the idea of stages. That is to say, the religious values stand at the top of a hierarchy of values. The sacred values—the values of holiness—are placed above even those of personality. And again, among the values of holiness, God's reality in Christ stands on the highest level, beyond the prophets and saints. Religion is the highest cultural value, and the Christian religion the highest sacred value. Obviously the concept of religion still dominates even this scheme. The series of stages permits each higher level to be grounded on the lower ones, both in terms of the image and in terms of the actual matter which this image is supposed to illustrate. The thinking here continues to be an ascending movement, from the bottom upwards. But at this point we must say that there are no stages leading to the Unconditional. The highest and the lowest are equidistant from the Unconditional.

Scholz replaces the theory of stages, whose medieval Catholic origin is evident, with the idea of the ethical-cultural personality, an idea clearly rooted in Protestantism. Religion is a reality independent of the rest of the spiritual life and can be either present or lacking. But if it is present, the norm for its evaluation is its capacity to be experienced by the contemporary cultured man, i.e., by the ethically and spiritually-formed personality. Of the experienceable religions, however, only three are finally taken into consideration: Christianity, pantheism and mysticism. It is, nevertheless, a complete contradiction of the unconditionality of the Unconditional to make its nature and scope dependent upon a particular state of ethical-spiritual personality or upon a specific cultural situation. All these ideas still come from a way of thinking that looks not to the Unconditional, but to the conditioned, in order to provide a norm for the Unconditional. They have not been able to expunge the [destructive] spirit of the concept of religion. Yet is there any way in which it can be expunged? Or is it the fate of philosophy of religion to be possessed by it? Is it the fate of human history to have the capacity for only the one or the other, religion or philosophy of religion?

3. The Conquest of the Concept of Religion

The decisive objection we have raised against previous philosophy of religion is that it founds the Unconditional upon the conditioned, either by co-ordinating them or, since this is intolerable, by assimilating the Unconditional into the conditioned. A philosophy of religion that wishes to do justice to the nature of the Unconditional must apprehend the Unconditional in everything conditioned as that which grounds both itself and the conditioned. The conditioned is the medium in and through which the Unconditional is apprehended. To this medium belongs, likewise, the perceiving subject. It, too, never appears as something that provides the ground, but rather as the place where the Unconditional becomes manifest within the conditioned. Consequently, one must make a distinction in principle between the meaning of statements about the Unconditional and those about the conditioned. But since every statement as such is expressed in the subject-object mode, and hence in the forms of the conditioned, statements about the Unconditional must, to be sure, utilize these forms. But this must occur in such a way that their inadequacy becomes evident, i.e., they must bear the form of systematic paradox.

a. Under domination by the concept of religion the self's certainty of itself is the basis for certainty of God. But two factors are contained in the self-certainty of the ego: the unconditionality of an apprehension of reality that lies beyond subject and object, and the participation of the subjective self in this unconditional reality which supports it. The self is the medium of the unconditional apprehension of reality, and as medium it participates in the certainty of that which it mediates. Still, it participates only as a medium; it is not that which upholds, but rather that which is upheld. The possibility exists for the ego to experience its self-certainty in such a way that the unconditional relation to reality contained within it stands in the foreground. This is the *a priori* religious mode of self-apprehension. On the other hand, the possibility exists for the ego to experience its self-certainty in such a manner that its relation to its own being stands in the foreground. This is the *a priori* unreligious mode of self-apprehension. In the first case, the self penetrates, so to speak, through the form of its consciousness to the ground of reality upon which it is based. In the second type, this underlying ground remains, to be sure, effective—without it there could be no self-certainty—but it is not touched upon; the self remains in its detached state, it settles for the *form* of consciousness. One can properly call this second position unreligious, but only with regard to its intention and not with regard to its outcome. There is no consciousness unreligious in substance, though it can certainly be so in intention. Every act of self-apprehension contains, as its foundation within reality, the relation to the Unconditional, but this relation is not in every case intended. The two states of consciousness are differentiated accordingly.

The statement that the certainty of the Unconditional is apprehended in self-certainty is paradoxical, for though it has a theoretical form, it is anything but theoretical in content. When it is said that the self grasps within itself the Unconditional as the basis of its own self-certainty, the opposition of subject and object is contained in the very form of this statement. But the import of the statement stands in direct contradiction to that, for the Unconditional is neither object nor subject, but rather the presupposition for every possible antithesis of subject and object. For this reason, apprehension of the Unconditional also stands prior to every theoretical judgment; and in its foundation as well as its consequences, it is independent of every theoretical certainty. Whether the spirit's intention is religious or unreligious is a matter of theoretical indifference, since the Unconditional is certainly the supporting ground of every theoretical judgment, and can be an absolute presupposition but never an object of theory. If nevertheless it becomes an object—and it must if anything is to be said about it at all—then the following statement necessarily has a paradoxical form: God-certainty is the certainty of the Unconditional contained in and grounding the self-certainty of the ego. Certainty of God is in this way utterly independent of any other presuppositional certainty. Both the self and its religion are subordinated to the Unconditional; they first become possible through the Unconditional. For this reason, there can be absolutely no certainty in which the certainty of God is not *implicite* present. Whether, however, it is likewise present *explicite* constitutes the decisive religious distinction. Objectively considered, all consciousness is related to God; but subjectively, consciousness can be God-less. Thus there is no way from the self to God, but there is, in terms of directedness rather than substance, a way from God to the self. Once one has embarked on this way, one can never go back. Only the breakthrough or eruption of the ground implicitly present in all self-consciousness through the autonomous forms of consciousness can free him from the compulsive flight from God. Religion calls this breakthrough "grace." Religion is aware that no theoretical pointing to the ground of all theory can make the Unconditional alive within consciousness. For theory makes the Unconditional into an object, i.e., precisely what it is not.

b. Under domination by the concept of religion the reality of God is grounded upon the reality of the world. Admittedly, every actuality exists in the forms of objectivity, of which one is existence itself. At the same time, however, within every actuality there is something unconditionally real to be grasped. This unconditionally real is not defined by the forms of objects and has, therefore, likewise no existence. Where the spirit directs itself upon the world and its contents in such a way that it brings to awareness the impulse of unconditionality implicit in all things, there it is directed toward God. This power of unconditional reality in every conditioned actuality is that which is the supporting ground in every thing (*Ding*), its very root of being, its absolute seriousness, its unfathomable depth, and its holiness. It is the import of its reality as distinguished from its accidental form.

All objective thinking must be strictly excluded here. We are not dealing with an object to be found either alongside things, or above or within them. The material-objective (*Gegenständlichen*) is not under consideration here at all, but rather the primordial (*Urständlichen*) as such, that which is exempt from all form, including that of existence. But here again it is the case that every statement is expressed in a material-objective form, and therefore is true only as a broken, paradoxical statement.

Thus, in respect to its form the statement "God is" is theoretical. No classification according to levels can change this, since God is thereby brought into the order of the world of objects. This pigeon-holing of God, however, is atheism. If the statement "God is" is likewise theoretical in its import, then it destroys the divinity of God. Meant as paradox, however, it is the necessary expression for the affirmation of the Unconditional, for it is not possible to direct oneself toward the Unconditional apart from objectification. By virtue of these considerations both deism and pantheism are overcome. Deism, which is not simply the orientation of a given historical period but an element in every representation of God, i.e., that point at which God is objectified and made finite, and which generally appears wherever the paradoxical meaning of divine being is no longer apprehended, is overcome. Pantheism, which, because the Unconditional is apprehensible within every actuality, equates the Unconditional with the universal form of materiality, i.e., with the world, is likewise overcome. It remains fixed upon an objective form, namely, the universal form of objective reality, and does not realize that the Unconditional is as far removed from the totality as it is from the individual. What is called for is a theism that has nothing in common with the customary semi–deism of the churches, a theism that says simply that the Unconditional is—the Unconditional.

There is no theoretical necessity for this attitude either. It is possible to focus one's attention upon the system of conditioned realities and to affirm it in this its character, as the autonomous self does. It is possible to disregard the relation to the unconditionally real inherent in everything that is, and to regard only the existence and form of objective reality, for everything in the world has the form of existence as well as of objectivity. This is possible without any theoretical reservation, since the Unconditional is at no time and at no point an object of theoretical contention. On the basis of theory it can be neither defended nor rejected. Nor does it venture into the arena of conflict over existential judgments, over questions of existence (*Dasein*) or non-existence (*Nichtsein*). If by renouncing the reality of God, however, one has once arrived at a reality of the world which is by intention independent of the divine—in substance, it can never be so—then there is no way back to the reality of God. For God is either the beginning or he does not exist.

c. Under domination by the concept of religion, religion is founded upon culture, either as a separate cultural function or as the synthesis of the cultural functions. This is fully analogous to the deistic and pantheistic conception of God. Yet there is a function of the spirit which neither stands alongside the other functions nor is their unity, but rather comes to expression in and through them, namely, the function of unconditionality. It is the root function, that function in which the spirit breaks through all of its forms and penetrates to its ground. For that reason it is not (properly) a form of the spirit and can only paradoxically be called a function. Phenomenologically expressed, there is a class of acts which originates out of a depth in which the contrast between one act and another is transcended. Consequently, the acts of this category can only take on a specific character by breaking into the medium of consciousness. Essentially, however, this is nothing other than the relation to the Unconditional inherent in every act. There is, therefore, no special religious function *along-side* the logical, aesthetic, ethical and social functions; nor is it confined either in *one* of them or in the *unity* of them all. It is rather that which breaks through each and all of them, and it is the reality, the unconditional significance of each of them. Just as things are the medium of the Unconditional in the world, so culture is the medium of the Unconditional in the life of the spirit.

On this basis we most emphatically reject the view that through religion a new value is introduced into a system of values. There are no values of holiness as such. The Holy is rather that which gives the values their value, the conditionality of their validity and the absoluteness of their relation to reality. Philosophy of religion is, therefore, under no condition a supplement to the philosophy of the spirit (*Geistesphilosophie*) or to the philosophy of values. In this instance as well, the Unconditional does not enter into the discussion of conditioned realities. The quality of holiness or the function of unconditionality can be absent without causing the slightest change in the system of values. Granted, here as everywhere, it can only be absent with respect to intention and not with respect to substance. For if it were absent in substance, thinking would be without truth, intuition without reality, action without purpose, community without vitality. Its presence, however, need not be intended. The human spirit can concern itself with the autonomy of its functions, whose forms it penetrates throughout, but whose root in reality it fails to touch. Through an autonomous self the spirit can produce autonomous culture in an autonomous universe. In doing so, however, it has blocked its own way to God. Within the realm of autonomous culture there can be at best— religion.

It is at this point that the dialectic of the concept of religion is to be made fully clear. As soon as consciousness directs itself toward the Unconditional, the duality of act and object arises. Yet, a religious act is no special act; it can only become actual in other acts of the spirit. That is to say, it must give these other acts a formation in which their religious quality is visible, and that formation is paradox, i.e., the simultaneous affirmation and negation of autonomous form. Religious thinking—and intuitive perception is thus a mode of thinking—is a "perceiving" (*Anschauen*) in which the autonomous forms of thought and intuition are simultaneously employed and shattered. The same holds true for the moral and social forms.

Thus, in the presence of the Unconditional, knowing is inspiration, intuitive perception is mystery, acting is grace, and community is the kingdom of God. These are all paradoxical concepts, i.e., concepts that immediately lose their meaning when construed objectively. Understood as a sort of supernatural transmission of knowledge, inspiration becomes a plain contradiction; mystery, understood in the sense of a real material presence of the Unconditional within the conditioned, becomes a meaningless statement; grace, understood as a supernatural impartation of power, becomes ethical nonsense; and the kingdom of God, conceived as material grandeur, becomes a utopia of mechanistic thinking. In each case the paradox has been replaced by supernaturalism, i.e., the attempt to make a conditioned reality unconditional. But corresponding to supernaturalism there is always a naturalism which attempts to eliminate the Unconditional entirely.

Yet religion can do nothing other than work with these concepts. In order to make any statements at all, it must objectify. Its desire to make assertions is its holiness; the necessary objective character of all its assertions is its secularity. Only when religion sees through its own dialectic and gives all honor to the Unconditional, can it be justified. Where it fails to do this, religion debases the Unconditional and leads it within the arena of controversy concerning conditioned realities, where it must of necessity be overcome. Religion then becomes a cultural phenomenon that has lost all connection with the Unconditional, a way of thinking that no longer knows anything of inspiration as the breakthrough of unconditional reality, an intuition that has lost sense of the mystery of the ground within the forms of things, an acting that in the absence of grace has lapsed into law, a community that has become remote from the breakthrough of unconditional love. This is one possibility for religion. The other is a religion that has made supernatural laws of all these concepts, objectifying the paradox and rendering the Unconditional finite. Such is the state of the human spirit under the domination of the concept of religion. Conquering the spirit of that concept means the redemption of religion from the fate of objectification, redemption of culture from the fate of secularization, and the Unconditional breaking through every mode of relativization.

d. Under domination by the concept of religion, revelation is based upon the autonomous life of the spirit, whether this be in the sense of a revealed religion of reason or in the sense of a history of religion. In this way the absolute divine act becomes a relative evolution of man's religious spirit. Religion, however, does not seek religion, not even absolute religion, but rather it seeks redemption, revelation, salvation, regeneration, life and consummation; it wants the unconditionally Real, it desires God. It calls true religion that in which God manifests himself, and false religion that in which he is sought in vain. But the concept of religion cannot acknowledge such distinctions, not even in the veiled form of experienceable versus non-experienceable religion. The concept of religion is a leveler, putting the divine and the human on the same plane. Thus, whenever one particular religion is made unconditional, this is already a result of the concept of religion, already a relativizing of the Unconditional. As religion, every religion is relative, for every religion objectifies the Unconditional. As revelation, however, every religion can be absolute, for revelation is the breakthrough of the Unconditional in its unconditionality. Every religion is absolute to the degree that it is revelation, i.e., insofar as the Unconditional manifests itself within it as something unconditional, in contrast to everything relative that belongs to it as religion.

Yet it is the character of every living religion that it carries within itself a constant opposition to its own religiosity. Protest against objectification is the pulse beat of religion. Only where this is lacking does it no longer contain anything absolute. It has then become mere religion, completely human. The typical protest of living religion against its objectification has taken three forms: mysticism, predestination, and grace. *Mysticism* penetrates to the paradoxical meaning of every statement about the Unconditional. It seeks unity with that which is absolutely objective, with the abyss, with the transcendent (*Überseienden*), with pure "nothingness" (*Nichts*). It knows, furthermore, that this union can only be brought about by the Unconditional; it knows that it is a matter of grace. Nevertheless, it prepares itself to become worthy of grace, and for that end it both utilizes the forms of religion and creates forms of its own. It never leaves the soil of religion, and that is its limitation. *Predestination,* on the other hand, ascribes all activity on behalf of the salvation of the individual and of humanity to God. Neither religion nor the church is a precondition for election or the kingdom of God. They are at best divinely ordained mediations of those ends. As a result of this, their significance diminishes; and because the divine decree takes place in secret, all human religious activities and representations are devaluated and soon approach the point where they completely cease and pass over into secular cultural activity. That is the danger of placing the religious element entirely within the sphere of the hidden and absolute. The third form is *concrete grace*. To be sure, mysticism and predestination also live from grace. However, concrete grace also locates salvation completely in the Unconditional, but in its concrete, historical self-manifestation and not in its abyss, not in its hidden will. Consequently, it issues in a vigorous affirmation of the religious and ecclesiastical media, of the mediator and means of revelation, of prayer and living fellowship with God. But this view almost inevitably goes astray at this point by elevating these media into an absolute status and thus the revelation of grace becomes a religion of the means of grace.

Each of these three forms in which religion is overcome within religion is characterized by the same dialectic as religion itself. They can set themselves in the place of God. For that reason it is likewise false to make these forms into an absolute religion. They are forms of expression for the absolute element in every living religion, but as soon as they become forms of religion they themselves become relative. Absolute religion is to be found in all religions. True religion exists wherever the Unconditional is affirmed as the Unconditional, and religion is abolished through its presence.

The presence of true religion is generally hidden. It becomes manifest "now and then" in the form of the great mystical or prophetic reactions against mere religion. The degree to which a religion is open to such reactions determines its relative rank. Absolute religion is never an objective fact, but rather a momentary and vital breakthrough of the Unconditional. God himself demonstrates what absoluteness is by shattering the claim of religion to absoluteness, not through skepticism or the history of religion, but by revealing his unconditionality, before which all religion is nothing.

Thus here, too, the sustaining element is the Unconditional, and God's activity is the substance without which religion cannot exist. But religion can ignore this. It can consciously or unconsciously leave this substance untouched and devote attention to its own autonomous forms. Religion can become autonomous and self-sufficient, far removed from God. And it can consummate the idolatry by calling itself absolute religion.

The justifiability of the four objections religion raises against philosophy of religion has now been acknowledged. But it does not follow from this that philosophy of religion must be abolished for the sake of religion. Instead, an attempt has been made to establish a philosophy of religion upon the demands contained within these objections, i.e., a philosophy of religion that starts with the Unconditional rather than the conditioned, with God rather than religion. The fate of philosophy of religion, as well as the attitude of the life of the spirit toward religion, does not rest upon the success or failure of this present endeavor, but rather upon the success or failure of some such undertaking in general. We confront the following alternatives: either the dissolution (*Aufhebung*) of religion through culture, or the breakthrough of the unconditionally real as the ground or reality of the whole of culture in all its functions. The manner in which this breakthrough could be effected within the scientific realm should be indicated by the thoughts expressed in this essay. There can be no doubt for me concerning the objective (viz. breakthrough), but the form of these ideas presented here is simply an attempt and nothing more.

4. The Dialectic of Autonomy

Everything said thus far had basically one goal. It was to prepare the way for a state of mind in which the self-certainty of the conditioned was shattered before the certainty and reality of the Unconditional. My main concern was not to solve a theoretical problem, but rather to indicate a spiritual situation towards which, I am convinced, the course of spiritual development fatefully moves. Thus it is all the more needful to render an account of the methods of thought which we have employed. Two points must be considered: a particular method and a particular philosophy of history, or a logical presupposition and a metaphysical one.

a. The method employed throughout the essay but especially in the analysis of self-certainty, may be described as a critical-intuitive method. It proceeds from the conviction that neither the critical nor the intuitive method alone is capable of solving the central problem of philosophy of religion, and hence also of philosophy of culture—namely, the question concerning the ultimate meaning and reality of every actual thing. The critical method fails because under no circumstances can it get beyond the forms of the given to the given itself. The intuitive method fails because it is so immersed in every possible given that it must completely disregard the form of givenness. The critical method cannot grasp the "what-ness" of things; the intuitive method cannot grasp their "that-ness." In considering the problem of reality the critical method loses the reality itself, and becomes formalism. Because of its immediate intuition of what is actual the intuitive method loses sight of the problem of reality, and becomes romantic and reactionary. But the problem of the Unconditional is to determine the point where the distinction between existence and essence is transcended, and for that purpose the employment of these methods alongside each other is impossible. To approach that point it is absolutely imperative to have a method in which the other two are united, namely, a "critical-intuitive" method. When this demand has been fully realized, an adequate name for the method will also emerge. But it seems to me to consist essentially of the following elements: it finds its basis in the critical method, and starts from the functions of the spirit considered as the forms in which all things are given. It turns back upon itself, however, and sees that all these forms are empty unless they are filled with the import of something unconditionally real which cannot be grasped either by any single form or by the totality of all forms. That which gives meaning to all things is not itself a meaning, nor is it the totality or even the infinity of meaning. That which is the "real" (*Reale*) in all things is not itself a reality, nor is it the totality or even the infinity of the real. The perception of this, however, is no longer a matter of criticism but of intuition. Where criticism establishes its boundary concepts (which are testimony to its own limitedness), there intuition perceives the unconditionally real that constitutes the root of reality from which all criticism lives. Indeed, it intuits this root not beyond those boundaries set by criticism, but precisely in the midst of the critically defined realm. Intuition is the method appropriate to paradox, to the constant breakthrough and annulment of form for the sake of the reality within it. Neither formlessness nor domination by an alien form can be tolerated to break through the critically defined form, for that would be a renunciation of all methodical inquiry, and hence of philosophy. Rather, in full affirmation of autonomous critical form, the import of the Unconditional is to break forth and shatter form, not formlessly but paradoxically. Life within this highest of tensions is life from God. Intuition of this infinite paradox is thinking about God;

and if it is methodically developed, it becomes philosophy of religion or theology. Of course, no one can be systematically compelled to employ this method, as in the case of the merely critical method. It is possible to live and think without discerning the roots out of which one does so. It is possible to make the Unconditional into a boundary concept, or an ideal concept, or something similar; it is possible to push it to the side and to remain within the autonomy of mere form. All this is possible, but the result is self-destructive. That leads us to the second point, concerning philosophy of history.

b. A spiritual situation may be termed "theonomous" in which all forms of the spiritual life are an expression of the unconditionally real breaking through within them. They are forms, in other words, laws, and therefore, theo*nomous*. But they are forms whose meaning does not lie within themselves, laws which grasp that which breaks through every law, and therefore, *theo*nomous. In certain periods, e.g., the medieval period in the West, this spiritual situation was almost actualized. As soon as a theonomous period approaches its end, it attempts to preserve those forms which were once the adequate expression of its import. These forms, however, have become empty. If they are maintained through authority, heteronomy results. Heteronomy always emerges out of a religion that has lost God and has become mere religion. But then autonomy springs up in opposition to heteronomy. It is always in reaction against that autonomy of mere religion which seeks to subject all of culture to its heteronomy. The autonomy of religion over against God produces the autonomy of culture over against religion. The close of the Middle Ages is typical of this spiritual situation. Autonomous culture is justifiably opposed to religion. Logical form has the right to oppose an erstwhile paradoxical form that has been divested of its meaning and now, as mere contradiction, seeks to overthrow the claims of logic. In this conflict the victory of autonomous form, whether in the logical or aesthetic, the legal or ethical sphere, has been determined from the outset. This victory signifies an insight into the objective forms of things; it signifies an exact scientific discipline, and technical-rational control of the world.

The victory is, nevertheless, a costly one. The right of autonomy over against heteronomy becomes unjustified over against theonomy, for autonomous form is law. Things can be made technical and rational through law, but it is impossible to live under the law. When the Unconditional is grasped only as the unconditional validity of logical, ethical or aesthetic form, life is destroyed. For the Unconditional is then a judge that condemns every individual form because it fails to fulfill the law, because it fails to attain the conditionality of the Unconditional. For this reason, every period of autonomy necessarily breaks down. By means of its formal unconditionality it can rationalize and destroy everything living, but it cannot create a single content of life. It loses truth and remains in the empty form of identity; it loses personality and remains in the empty form of "thou shalt"; it loses beauty and remains in the empty form of synthesis; it loses community and remains in the empty form of equality. But every desperate struggle to fulfill these forms, in the logical as in the ethical realm, in thought as well as action, only expresses the tragedy of autonomy.

This struggle is overpowering in magnitude, and this tragedy shakes the very foundations. Out of these times of struggle great individual cultural creations have issued. Yet such periods terminate in a vacillation between pretentious rationalism and despairing skepticism in the logical sphere, and between Pharisaism and lawlessness in the ethical sphere. Autonomy breaks apart into legalism and antinomianism. Life remains viable only for those who evade the great tensions of the human spirit and utilize the autonomous forms for technical and tactical purposes in science and economics, in politics and art. They already have their reward; but the reward of the spirit that perseveres is the Unconditional breaking through all forms, not as law but as grace, as fate, as an immediately given overpowering reality—as, for example, it was granted to antiquity in the dual form of Neoplatonic mysticism on the logical level and Christianity on the ethical.

The theme of cultural history is the struggle between theonomy and autonomy. Theonomy is victorious so long as it remains a living breakthrough, so long as the paradoxical is experienced as paradox. But it is the fate of theonomy ever and again to transform the living paradox into an objective contradiction. Then out of the struggle against this heteronomous end of theonomy there emerges victoriously an autonomy of form, only to come in due course to its own fate of dissolution. This philosophy of history is not to be understood in a mere seriation sense, for this conflict rages in every moment of the history of the spirit. But the victory or defeat of one or the other of these spiritual possibilities *does* produce a sequence or philosophy of history which applies not only to the cross-section of single historical moments or periods, but also to the longitudinal development of history.

We have observed the struggle of autonomy and theonomy within the philosophy of religion. That is the place where the conflict is most visible. In its development philosophy of religion is itself a part of this struggle. It can be *philosophy* only because the autonomous development has provided it with forms. But it can be philosophy of *religion* only when theonomy provides it with import, with rootage in the Unconditional. But that can happen only if it escapes domination by that concept which is the characteristic symbol of an autonomous period that has turned away from God, namely, the concept of religion. That can happen only if philosophy of religion perceives that God and not religion is the beginning and end, the center of all things. It can happen only if it realizes that every religion and every philosophy of religion loses God the moment it forsakes this ground: *Impossibile est, sine deo discere deum.* God is known only through God!

III

On the Idea
of a Theology of Culture*

1. Theology and Religious Philosophy

In the empirical sciences one's own standpoint is something that must be overcome. Reality is the criterion by which what is right is measured, and reality is one and the same. As between two contradictory standpoints, only one can be right, or both can be wrong. The progress of scientific experience must decide between them. It has decided that the earth is a body in space and not a flat, floating plate, and that the five Books of Moses stem from various sources and not from Moses himself. Standpoints opposed to this are wrong. Scientific progress has not yet decided who is the author of the Epistle to the Hebrews. Among the various hypotheses only one, or none, is correct.

The situation is different in the systematic cultural sciences; *here the standpoint of the systematic thinker belongs to the heart of the matter itself*. It is a moment in the history of the develop-

* Translated by William Baillie Green. For their helpful suggestions the translator wishes to thank Mr. Walter Bernhardt and Professors Ria Stavrides, Wener Rode, Joan Stambaugh, and Charles W. Fox.

ment of culture; it is a concrete historical realization of an idea of culture; it not only perceives but also creates culture. Here the alternative "right or wrong" loses its validity, for there is no limit to the number of attitudes which the spirit can adopt toward reality. There is a Gothic and a baroque style in aesthetics; a Catholic and a modern Protestant dogmatic theology; a romantic and a puritanical code of ethics; but in none of these pairs of alternatives is it possible simply to call one right and the other wrong. Therefore it is also impossible to form useful universal concepts of cultural ideas. The true nature of religion or art cannot be learned through abstract reasoning. Abstraction destroys what is essential, the concrete forms, and necessarily neglects any future concretizations. *Every universal concept in cultural science is either useless or a normative concept in disguise;* it is either an alleged description of something that does not exist or an expression of a standpoint; it is a worthless shell or it is a creative act. A standpoint is expressed by an individual; but if it is more than individual arbitrariness, if it is a creative act, it is also, to a greater or lesser degree, a creative act of the circle in which the individual moves. This circle, with its peculiar spiritual quality, has no existence apart from the cultural groups that surround it and the creative acts of the past on which it rests. Thus, in the same way even the most individual standpoint is firmly embedded in the ground of the objective spirit, the mother soil from which every cultural creation springs. From this soil the concrete standpoint derives the universal forms of spirit. And viewed from there, it finds its own concrete limitation through the ever narrower circles and historical components of concrete spiritual quality, until, by its own creative self-expression it develops the new individual and unique synthesis of universal form and concrete content. There are three forms of nonempirical cultural science which correspond to this: philosophy of culture, which is concerned with the universal forms, the a priori of all culture; the philosophy of the history of cultural values, which, through the abundance of concretizations, constitutes the transition from the universal forms to one's own individual standpoint and by so doing justifies the latter; and finally, the normative science of culture, which provides the concrete standpoint with a systematic expression.

Thus the following distinctions must be made: between the philosophy of art, i.e., a phenomenology of art, and a presentation of art within a philosophy of value concerned with the essence or value of "art" on the one hand, and "aesthetics," i.e., a systematic and normative presentation of what must be considered as beautiful, on the other hand. Or between moral philosophy—which asks "What is morality?"—and normative ethics, which asks "What is moral?" The same distinction must be made between philosophy of religion on the one hand and theology on the other. *Theology is thus the concrete and normative science of religion.* This is the sense in which the concept is used here, and in my opinion it is the only sense in which it is entitled to be used in any scholarly context. By this means two allegations are refuted. First, theology is not the science of one particular object, which we call God, among others; the *Critique of Reason* put an end to this kind of science. It also brought theology down from heaven to earth. Theology is a part of science of religion, namely the systematic and normative part. Second, theology is not a scientific presentation of a special complex of revelation. This interpretation presupposes a concept of a supernaturally authoritative revelation; but this concept has been overcome by the wave of religious-historical insights and the logical and religious criticism of the conception of supernaturalism.

It is therefore the task of theology, working from a concrete standpoint, to draw up a normative system of religion based on the categories of philosophy of religion, with the individual standpoint being related to the standpoint of the respective confession, the universal history of religion, and the cultural-historical standpoint in general. This is no hidden rationalism, for it recognizes the concrete religious standpoint. Nor is it hidden supernaturalism, such as may still be found even in our historical-critical school of thought, for it is the breaking down of all the authoritarian limitations upon the individual standpoint by means of a philosophy of history. It is oriented to Nietzsche's notion of the "creative" on the basis of Hegel's concept of "objective-historical spirit."

One final word on the relation between a philosophy of culture and a normative systematization of culture: they belong together and each exercises an influence over the other. Not only is theology oriented to philosophy of religion, but the reverse is also true. As indicated at the outset, any universal philosophical concept is empty unless it is at the same time understood to be a normative concept with a concrete basis. Accordingly, this does not constitute the difference between philosophy and the science of norms, but the fact that each works in a different direction. Philosophy provides universal, a priori categorical thought forms on the widest empirical basis and in systematic relationship with other values and essential concepts. The normative sciences provide each cultural discipline with its content, with what is peculiar to it, with what is to be regarded as valid within the specific system.

Out of the power of a concrete, creative realization the highest universal concept gains its validity, full of content and yet comprehensive in form; and out of a highest universal concept the normative system acquires its objective scientific significance. In every useful universal concept there is a normative concept; and in every creative "norm" concept there is a universal concept. This is the dialectic of the systematic science of culture.

2. Culture and Religion

Traditionally, systematic theology has included theological ethics as well as dogmatics. Modern theology usually divides the system into apologetics, dogmatics, and ethics. What is this peculiar kind of knowledge which assumes a place beside the general philosophical subject of ethics under the name of theological ethics? To this one can give various answers. One can say that philosophical ethics is concerned with the nature of morality and not with its norms; in which case the two differ from each other as do moral philosophy and normative ethics. But why should normative ethics be theological ethics? Philosophy, or better the science of culture, cannot refrain from producing a system of normative ethics of its own. Insofar as both now claim to be valid, we would then have admitted in principle the existence of the old double truth in the sphere of ethics. But one can also say: the moral life likewise tends to become concrete, and in ethics, too, there must be a standpoint that is not only the standpoint of an individual but also stems from a concrete ethical community in historical contexts. The church is such a community.

This answer is correct wherever the church is the dominating cultural community or wherever culture is under the leadership of the church and not only ethics but also science, art, and social life are controlled, censored, kept within limits, and systematized by the church. In Protestant areas, however, the church has long ago abandoned any claim to do this. It recognizes an overlapping cultural community outside the church, where the individual viewpoint is rooted in the contemporary viewpoint of the cultural community in general. There is no more room for a system of ethics, aesthetics, science, or sociology based on theological principles than there would be for a German or Aryan or bourgeois system of the same kind, although these concretions naturally play an important part in the actual shaping of the individual standpoint. Once a secular culture has been recognized in principle by the church, there is no longer any question of a theological system of ethics—nor of a theological system of logic, aesthetics, and sociology.

My assertion now is the following: *What was essentially intended in the theological system of ethics can only be realized by means of a theology of culture applying not only to ethics but to all the functions of culture. Not a theological system of ethics, but a theology of culture.* This calls for a few remarks on the relation of culture to religion. Religion has the peculiarity of not being attributable to any particular psychic function. None of the theories advanced either by Hegel, who assigned religion to the theoretical sphere of the mind, or by Kant, who assigned it to the practical sphere, or by Schleiermacher, who assigned it to the realm of feeling, has survived. The last theory is the one nearest to the truth, inasmuch as it signifies the indifference of the genuinely religious realm toward its cultural expressions. But feeling accompanies *every* cultural experience without necessarily justifying its being described as religious. However, if a *definite* feeling is meant, then with this certainty a theoretical or practical element is already given. Religion is not a feeling; it is an attitude of the spirit in which practical, theoretical, and emotional elements are united to form a complex whole.

In my opinion, the following is the way of systematizing which most nearly approaches the truth. If we now divide all cultural functions into those through which the spirit absorbs the object into itself—i.e., intellectual and aesthetic functions, grouped together as theoretical or intuitive—and those through which the spirit tries to penetrate into the object and mold it after itself—i.e., the individual and the socioethical functions (including law and society), which is the practical group, we find that religion can become operative only in relation to a theoretical or practical attitude. The religious potency, i.e., a certain quality of consciousness, is not to be confused with the religious act, i.e., an independent theoretical or practical act containing that quality.

The connection between religious principle and cultural function now enables a specifically religious-cultural sphere to emerge: a religious perception—myth or dogma; a sphere of religious aesthetics—the cultus; a religious molding of the person—sanctification; a religious form of society—the church, with its special canon law and communal ethic. In forms like these, religion is actualized; the religious principle only exists in connection with cultural functions outside the sphere of religion. The religious function does not form a principle in the life of the spirit beside others; the absolute character of all religious consciousness would break down barriers of that kind. But the religious principle is actualized in all spheres of spiritual or cultural life. This remark, however, seems to have set new boundaries. In every sphere of cultural life there is now a special circle, a special sphere of influence of "the religious." How are these spheres to be defined? Here indeed is the field of the great cultural conflicts between church and state, between the religious community and society, between art and cultic form, between science and dogma—conflicts which occupied the first centuries of the modern era and which have not yet entirely ceased. No conflict is possible as long as the cultural functions are held by a heteronomy dominated by religion; and it is overcome as soon as the cultural functions have won complete autonomy. But what happens then to religion? The autonomy of the cultural life is threatened, and even abolished, as long as science stands in any way side by side with dogma; or society side by side with a "community"; or the state side by side with a church—all of them claiming definite spheres for themselves alone. For through this a double truth, a double morality, and a double justice come into being, and one out of each pair has its origin not in the legitimacy of the cultural function concerned but in an alien kind of legitimacy dictated by religion. This double existence must be abolished at all costs; it is intolerable as soon as it enters consciousness, for it destroys consciousness.

The solution can only be found through the concept of religion. Without offering proof, for that would mean writing a miniature philosophy of religion, I shall present the concept of religion I presuppose here. Religion is directedness toward the Unconditional. Through existing realities, through values, through personal life, the meaning of unconditional reality becomes evident; before which every particular thing and the totality of all particulars—before which every value and the system of values—before which personality and community are shattered in their own self-sufficient being and value. This is not a new reality, alongside or above other things: that would only be a thing of a higher order which would again fall under the No. On the contrary, it is precisely through things that that reality is thrust upon us which is at one and the same time the No and the Yes to every thing. It is not a being, nor is it the substance or totality of beings; it is—to use a mystical formula—that which is above all beings which at the same time is the absolute Nothing and the absolute Something. But even the predicate "is" already disguises the facts of the case, since we are here dealing not with a reality of existence, but with a reality of meaning, and that indeed is the ultimate and deepest meaning—reality which shakes the foundation of all things and builds them up anew.

At this point it now becomes clear without further reference that one cannot speak of special religious spheres of culture in the true sense of the term. If it is the nature of fundamental religious experience to negate the *entire* cognitive sphere and affirm it through negation, then there is no longer any place for a special religious cognition, a special religious object, or special methods of religious epistemology. The conflict between dogma and science is overcome. Science is in full possession of its autonomy, and there is no possibility of a rule of heteronomy exercised by religion; but in exchange for this, science as a whole is subordinated to the "theonomy" of a fundamental religious experience which is paradoxical. The same holds good of ethics. It is impossible for a special code of personal or communal ethics in relation to the religious object to exist side by side with an individual or social code of ethics. Ethics, too, is purely autonomous, entirely free of all religious heteronomy and yet "theonomous" as a whole in the sense of the fundamental religious experience. The possibilities of conflict are radically eliminated. By that the relation of religion to culture is clarified in principle. The specifically religious spheres of culture have in principle ceased to exist. The question of what importance may still be attached to them can only be decided after the question of the meaning of a theology of culture has been answered.

3. Theology of Culture

Various references have been made in the last few pages to an autonomy and theonomy of cultural values. We have to follow these up still further: that is, I would like to propose the hypothesis that the autonomy of cultural functions is grounded in their form, in the laws governing their application, whereas theonomy is grounded in their substance or import, that is, in the reality which by these laws receives its expression or accomplishment. The following law can now be formulated: The more the form, the greater the autonomy; the more the substance or import, the greater the theonomy. But one cannot exist without the other; a form that forms nothing is just as incomprehensible as substance without form. To attempt to grasp import disengaged from form would constitute a relapse into the worst kind of heteronomy; a new form would immediately come into being, now opposing the autonomous form and limiting it in its autonomy. The relation of import to form must be taken as resembling a line, one pole of which represents pure form and the other pole pure import. Along the line itself, however, the two are always in unity. The revelation of a predominant import consists in the fact that the form becomes more and more inadequate, that the reality, in its overflowing abundance, shatters the form meant to contain it; and yet this overflowing and shattering is itself still form.

The task of a theology of culture is to follow up this process in all the spheres and creations of culture and to give it expression. Not from the standpoint of form—that would be the task of the branch of cultural science concerned—but taking the import or substance as its starting point, as theology of culture and not as cultural systematization. The concrete religious experiences embedded in all great cultural phenomena must be brought into relief and a mode of expression found for them. It follows from this that in addition to theology as a normative science of religion, a theological method must be found to stand beside it in the same way that a psychological and a sociological method, etc., exist alongside systematic psychology. These methods are universal; they are suited to any object; and yet they have a native soil, the particular branch of knowledge in which they originated. This is equally true of the theological method, which is a universal application of theological questioning to all cultural values.

We have assigned to theology the task of finding a systematic form of expression for a concrete religious standpoint, on the basis of the universal concepts of philosophy of religion and by means of the classifications of philosophy of history. The task of theology of culture corresponds to this. It produces a general religious analysis of all cultural creations; it provides a historical-philosophical and typological classification of the great cultural creations according to the religious substance realized in them; and it produces from its own concrete religious standpoint the ideal outline of a culture penetrated by religion. It thus has a threefold task, corresponding to the threefold character of the cultural-systematic sciences in general and the systematic science of religion in particular:

1. *General religious analysis of culture*
2. *Religious typology and philosophy of cultural history*
3. *Concrete religious systematization of culture*

Attention must be paid to two things in regard to the cultural-theological analysis. The first is the relation between form and substance. *Substance or import* is something different from content. By content we mean something objective in its simple existence, which by form is raised up to the intellectual-cultural sphere. By substance or import, however, we understand the meaning, the spiritual substantiality, which alone gives form its significance. We can therefore say: *Substance or import is grasped by means of a form and given expression in a content.* Content is accidental, substance essential, and form is the mediating element. The form must be appropriate to the content; so there is no opposition between the cultivation of form and the cultivation of content; it is rather that these two represent one extreme, and the cultivation of substance represents the other. The shattering of form through substance is identical with the loss of significance of content. Form loses its necessary relation to content because the content vanishes in the face of the preponderance of the substance. Through this, form acquires a quality of detachment, as of something floating freely in space; it is directly related to substance; it loses its natural and necessary relation to content; and it becomes form in a paradoxical sense by allowing its natural quality to be shattered by the substance. This is the first point to which attention must be paid; for it is precisely in the substance that the religious reality appears with its Yes and No to all things. And this is the second point: the relation between the Yes and the No, the relation and the force in which both find expression. There are innumerable possibilities here, because the relations and the reciprocal interactions are infinitely rich in possibilities.

But there is also a certain limitation: and this leads us to the second task assigned to theology of culture, the typological and historical-philosophical task. A limitation is given by the aforementioned image of the line with the poles of form and substance (or import) respectively. This image leads us to three decisive points representing the three fundamental types: the two poles and the central point where form and substance are in equilibrium. From this may be derived the following fundamental classifications for typology: the typically profane or secular and formal cultural creation; the typically religious-cultural creation in which the substance or import is predominant; and the typically well-balanced, harmonious, or classical cultural creation. This universal typology now leaves room for intermediate stages and transitions and is extraordinarily varied by reason of the different concrete forms of religion which it covers. If this doctrine of types is applied to the present and systematically related to the past, a historical-philosophical classification develops which then leads us directly to the third and, properly speaking, systematic task of theology of culture.

How far can the theologian of culture be at the same time a religious-cultural system-builder? The question has to be answered first from its negative side. It is impossible as far as the form of the cultural functions is concerned; that would be a forbidden infringement and would amount to cultural heteronomy. It is possible only from the side of substance, but substance only attains cultural existence in forms; to this extent it must be said that the theologian of culture is not directly creative with regard to culture. The theologian of culture as such is not productive in the sphere of science, morals, jurisprudence, or art. But he adopts a critical, negative, and affirmative attitude toward autonomous productions on the basis of his concrete theological standpoint; he draws up with the material at hand a religious system of culture by separating this material and unifying it again in accordance with his theological principle. He can also go beyond the material at hand, but only in making demands and not in fulfillment; he can reproach the existing culture because he finds nothing in its creative acts which he can acknowledge as an expression of the living substance in himself; he can indicate in a very general way the direction in which he visualizes the realization of a truly religious system of culture, but he cannot produce the system himself. If he attempts to do so, he ceases to be a theologian of culture and becomes in one or more ways a creator of culture; but in so doing he steps over to the full and completely autonomous criticism of cultural forms, which often leads him with compelling force to goals quite different from those he wished to attain. Herein lies the limitation of the task of systematization assigned to the theologian of culture: but his universal significance also originates here. Far removed from every restriction to a special sphere, he can give expression from the standpoint of substance to the all-embracing unity of the cultural functions and demonstrate the relations that lead from one phenomenon of culture to another, through the substantial unity of the substance finding expression in them; he can thereby help, from the viewpoint of substance, to bring about the unity of culture in the same way that the philosopher helps from the viewpoint of pure forms and categories.

Cultural-theological tasks have often been posed and solved by theological, philosophical, literary, and political analysts of culture (e.g., Simmel); but the task as such has not been understood or its systematic meaning recognized. It has not been realized that in this context it is a matter of a cultural synthesis of the greatest importance, a synthesis that not only embraces the various cultural functions but also overcomes the culture-destroying opposition of religion and culture by a design for a religious system of culture in which the opposition of science and dogma is replaced by a science religious in itself; the distinction between art and forms of cultus is replaced by an art religious in itself; and the dualism of state and church is replaced by a type of state religious in itself, etc. The task of theology of culture is only understood if it is seen within so wide a scope. Some examples should serve to explain and lead further.

4. Cultural-Theological Analyses

In what follows I want to limit myself mainly to the first, or analytical, part of cultural-theological work, with occasional references to the second, or typological part, since I do not wish to introduce at this point a concrete theological principle without offering proof; that, however, would be necessary for the completion of the historical-philosophical and systematic task of theology of culture. One or two indications with regard to systematization, however, will make some appearance in the course of the analysis.

I begin with a cultural-theological consideration of art—to be precise, with the Expressionist school of art in painting, because it seems to me to offer a particularly impressive example of the above-mentioned relation between form and substance; and because these definitions were worked out partly under its influence.

To start with, it is clear that in Expressionism content has to a very great extent lost its significance, namely content in the sense of the external factuality of objects and events. Nature has been robbed of her external appearance; her uttermost depth is visible. But, according to Schelling, horror dwells in the depths of every living creature; and this horror seizes us from the work of the Expressionist painters, who aim at more than mere destruction of the form in favor of the fullest, most vital and flourishing life within, as Simmel thinks. In their work a form-shattering religious import is struggling to find form, a paradox that most people find incomprehensible and annoying; and this horror seems to me to be deepened by a feeling of guilt, not in the properly ethical sense, but rather in the cosmic sense of the guilt of sheer existence. Redemption, however, is the transition of one individual existence into the other, the wiping out of individual distinction, the mysticism of love achieving union with all living things.

This art therefore expresses the profoundest No and Yes; but the No, the form-destroying element, seems to me still to be predominant, although this is not what the artists, with their passionate will toward a new and absolute Yes, intend.

Many of the remarks made by these artists confirm the existence of a strong religious passion struggling for expression. It is no accident that in the lively debates carried on about these pictures, the enthusiastic representatives of Expressionism make constant references to philosophy and religion and even to the Bible itself. The religious meaning of this art is to a large extent consciously affirmed by its representatives.

And now for an example taken from philosophy. The autonomous forms of knowledge achieve perfect clarity in the Neo-Kantian school. Here we have a truly scientific—and unreligious —philosophy. Form rules absolutely. There are contemporary attempts to go beyond this, but that is harder in this field than in any other; during the idealistic period the experience of reality had engulfed the form too brutally. Not only that: Neo-Kantianism had forged for itself a new form, which in the name of intuition opposed the autonomous forms of knowledge. This was not a struggle between the different fields of knowledge; it was the old struggle between a particular religious mode of cognition and a profane or secular one. It was a piece of heteronomy which science was compelled to counteract, and did counteract, most vigorously. If now a new movement toward intuition succeeds in gaining influence when the fight against the materialistic shadow of idealism has been completely won, then a mistrust on the part of science is understandable, but not necessary. For a new intuitive method can never attempt to compete with the autonomous methods of science; it can only find an opening where the substance itself shatters the form of these methods and where the way into the realm of the metaphysical opens up. Metaphysics is nothing but the paradoxical attempt to fit into forms the experience of the Unconditional which is above and beyond all form; and if at this point we look back to Hegel, there still being no outstanding metaphysics at present, we find one of the most profound accounts of the unity of negation and affirmation, though it must be admitted that it has a strong optimistic tendency to raise affirmation above everything else. It does not include the experience of horror which is a fundamental part of Schelling's and Schopenhauer's work and should not be lacking in any modern metaphysics.

We come now to the sphere of practical values: first, to individual ethics. Nietzsche could serve as a splendid and characteristic example for a theology of culture in this sphere. His apparently totally antireligious orientation makes it particularly interesting to analyze, from the theological point of view, his doctrine of the shaping of the human personality. It should now be recognized that the opposition between the ethics of virtue and the ethics of grace is contained in his message and that, since Jesus' fight against the Pharisees and Luther's fight against Rome, there is hardly a parallel case where the personal forms of ethics are shattered by the substance with such violence.

"What is the greatest experience you can have? The hour in which you say: What does my virtue matter? It has not yet made me rage!" But the virtue that makes men rage is beyond virtue and sin. The theological sentence of destruction hangs mightily over each individual: "Thou shalt wish to consume thyself in thine own flame. How wouldst thou be new again if thou wert not first burned to ashes?" But almost at the same moment the affirmation arises, with unparalleled fervor and passion, whether as a sermon by the *Übermensch* or as a hymn to the marriage ring of rings, the ring of eternal return. This experience of reality which Nietzsche gained and contrasted with the personal goes so far beyond the individual-ethical form that he could be called the antimoralist *kat' exokēn* (par excellence), just as Luther has to be stigmatized as the great libertine by all those whose personal thinking takes place within the categories of virtue and reward.

171

From the standpoint of form, it is simply paradoxical how an overwhelming metaphysical substance deprives the ethical contents (norms) of significance, shatters the form adapted to them, and then still, of its own volition, presents within this shattered form a higher order of becoming a person than would have been possible within those other forms. The person who, according to Nietzsche, is beyond good and evil, is just "better" from the absolute viewpoint, even if he is "worse" from the relative, formal-ethical viewpoint, than the "good and righteous man." The former is "pious," whereas the righteous man is "impious."

In social ethics, it is the new mysticism of love now stirring everywhere that signifies a theonomous overcoming of the autonomous ethical forms without a relapse into the heteronomy of a specifically religious community of love. If you take the speeches of the idealistic socialists and communists, the poems of Rilke and Werfel, Tolstoi's new interpretation of the Sermon on the Mount —everywhere the formal system of ethics of reason and humanity oriented to Kant is being eliminated. Kant's formulae of ethical autonomy, his demand that man should do good for the sake of the good itself, and his law of universal validity are unassailable principles of autonomous ethics; and no interpretation of ethics as a divine commandment or of love as the overcoming of the law can be allowed to shake this foundation; but the content of love overflows the narrow cup of this form in an inexhaustible stream. The world that merely exists and is split up into individual beings is destroyed and experienced as an empty, unreal shell. The man who thinks in terms of the individual can never attain to love, for love is beyond the individual; the man who thinks in terms of the end to be attained does not know what love is: for love is pure experience of being, pure experience of reality. The man who tries to impose a limit or a condition upon love does not know that love is universal, cosmic, simply because it affirms and embraces everything that is real as something real.

Now we pass on to the theology of the state. This theology shows the substance embedded in the different forms of the state; it shows how this substance outgrows the form of the state, or, alternatively, how the form of the state stifles the substance. The rational theories of the state from which the autonomous state developed in the struggle against theocracy led to an abstract state floating above society, described in *Thus Spake Zarathustra* as "the coldest of all cold monsters." "Faith and love create a people, but the sword and a hundred greedy desires create the state" is a magnificent characterization of the unreligious power-state or utility-state. Nor does it help matters if we adorn this abstract, autonomous state with all the functions of culture and turn it into God on earth, as does Hegel; for then the spirit itself becomes a power-object or utility-object. The religious substance shatters the autonomous form of the state: that is the profoundest meaning of idealistic "anarchism," not to make way for a new theocracy but in favor of a theonomy built up from communities themselves and their spiritual substance. Even this is still a form of society—a state, but one created by negation, by the destruction of the autonomous form pertaining to a state; and this very paradox is the form of "anarchy." Such a state, built up from cultural communities, a "state" in the paradoxical sense of the term, is what must be termed "church" in the sense of the theology of culture: the universal human community, built up out of spiritual communities and bearing with it all cultural functions and their religious substance, with the great creative philosophers for its teachers, artists for its priests, the seers of a new ethic of the person and the community for its prophets, men who will lead it to new community goals for its bishops, leaders and recreators of the economic process for its deacons and almoners. For the economy, too, can be shattered in its pure autonomy and in its quality of being an end in itself, through the substance of the religious mysticism of love, which produces not for the sake of production but for the sake of the human being. Yet it does not curtail the process of production in accord with the principles of heteronomy, but directs it along the lines of theonomy as the universal form of the earlier, specifically ecclesiastical care of the poor which has been eliminated on socialist territory along with the concept of poverty.

With this we want to close the list of examples. I have given so many of them that they amount almost to the outline of a system of theology of culture. They will in any case serve to illustrate what is meant. At this point now the question could be raised why the whole of the work is limited to the analysis of culture and why nature (or technology) is excluded. The answer is that for us nature can only become an object through the medium of culture, if at all. For us, nature derives its sole importance from the functions of the spirit; and culture is conceived as both the subjective and objective embodiment of these functions. The essence of nature in itself is quite out of our reach, and we cannot even comprehend it sufficiently to be able to speak positively of such an essence. But as nature only becomes a reality to us through culture, we are justified in speaking exclusively of "cultural theology" and in rejecting a concept such as "natural theology." Any religious substance or import that may exist in nature lies in the cultural functions insofar as these are related to nature. The religious substance of a "landscape" is a religious-aesthetic phenomenon; the religious substance of a law of astronomy is a religious-scientific one. Technology can function in a religious way through aesthetic, socioethical, or legal interpretations; but in every case we find ourselves dealing with theology of culture, which unquestionably comprises the whole of nature and of technology. An independent natural theology would have to presuppose the existence of a mythology of "nature in itself," and that is unthinkable.

5. Theology of Culture and the Theology of the Church

We still have to deal with a question that has been postponed several times: What happens to the specifically religious culture, to dogma, cultus, sanctification, community, and church? How far does a special sphere of holiness still exist? The answer must be based on the relationship of polarity existing between the profane or secular and the religious aspects of the line of culture. In point of fact, they are never apart; but they are separated *in abstracto,* and this separation is the expression of a universal psychological need. In order to experience anything at all, we are perpetually compelled to separate things that in reality are bound up together, so that our conscious mind may become aware of them.

A specific religious culture must already have come into being before we can experience religious values in culture, or develop a theology of culture, or identify and label the religious elements. Church, cultus, and dogma must already have come into being, and not only that, before we can conceive of the state as church, or art as cultus, or science as theory of faith. To be able somehow to comprehend the Holy and experience it as distinct from the profane or secular, we must take it out of context and bring it into a special sphere of cognition, of worship, of love, and of organization. The profane or secular pole of culture—the exact sciences, formal aesthetics, formal ethics, the purely political and economic aspects—claims our whole attention if it is not balanced by the opposite pole; a universal profanation and desecration of life would be inevitable if no sphere of holiness existed to oppose and contradict it. This contradiction cannot be resolved as long as a distinction must be made between form and content, and as long as we are forced to live in the sphere of reflection and not in the sphere of intuition. This is one of the profoundest and most tragic contradictions of cultural life. But the importance of the progress made in recent centuries is revealed by the fact that we have learned the true nature of this conflict and have ceased to credit it with any real, fundamental significance, so that it has lost its residue of active power.

The relation of the theology of culture to the theology of the church is a consequence of this. Our whole development of this theme has taken culture and its forms as a starting point and has shown how culture as such receives a religious quality when substance or import flows into form, and how it finally produces a specifically religious-cultural sphere in order to preserve and heighten that religious quality. This sphere is one of teleo-logical, not independently logical, dignity. The church theologian now understands this sphere as the expression of a definite religious "concreteness," no longer derived from culture but with an independent history going back much farther than most other cultural creations. It has evolved its own forms, each with its separate history, its independence, and its continuity, in spite of all the influences exerted by autonomous forms of culture. Yes indeed, from its own nature it has exercised the very greatest influence on the evolution of these forms. That is an accurate statement of fact; but it is not adequate to decide the attitude that must be adopted toward theology of culture.

There are three possible attitudes that the church theologian can adopt toward culture. He can group all its aspects together under the heading of "world" and confront this group with the "kingdom of God," which is realized in the church. The result is that the specifically religious-cultural functions, insofar as they are exercised by the church, share in the "absoluteness" of the religious principle; and that there are absolute science, art forms, morality, etc.—i.e., those realized in the church, in its dogma, in its cultus, etc. Starting from this typically Catholic attitude, there is no possible road to a theology of culture.

The second possibility is the old Protestant attitude. Here church, cultus, and ethics are freed and seen in their relativity; but the cognitive tie, the idea of absolute knowledge as a supernatural revelation, is still retained. But since the period of the theology of the Enlightenment this position has been seriously shaken, for it is basically inconsistent; and the preference given to the intellectual sphere could no longer be justified, once the absoluteness of its only possible advocate, the church, had been allowed to lapse.

The task now facing present and future Protestant theology is to arrive at the third attitude. On the one hand, the distinction between religious potentiality and actuality, i.e., between religious principle and religious culture, will be strictly drawn and the character of "absoluteness" assigned only to the religious principle and not to any factor of the religious culture, not even that of its historical foundation. On the other hand, the religious principle will not be defined in purely abstract terms, nor will its concrete fulfillment be entrusted to every fleeting fashion of cultural development. Every effort, however, will be made to ensure the continuity of its concrete religious standpoint. Only if this attitude is adopted can there be any positive relation between theology of culture and the theology of the church.

In this relationship the church theologian is in principle the more conservative and the more selective, looking backward as well as forward. "The Reformation must continue" is his principle; but it is reformation and not revolution; for the substance of his concrete standpoint is preserved and the new mold must be adapted to the old one in every field.

The theologian of culture is not bound by any such considerations; he is a free agent in the living cultural movement, open to accept not only any other form but also any other spirit. It is true that he too lives on the basis of a definite concreteness, for *one can live* only in concreteness; but he is prepared at any time to enlarge and change this concreteness. As a theologian of culture, he has no interest in ecclesiastical continuity; and this of course puts him at a disadvantage as compared with the church theologian, since he is in danger of becoming a fashionable religious prophet of an uncertain cultural development divided against itself.

In consequence, the only relationship possible is one in which each is the complement of the other; and the best way of achieving this is through personal union, which is admittedly not always desirable, as types must be free to develop unhampered. In any case, a real opposition becomes impossible the moment the theologian of culture acknowledges the necessity of the concrete standpoint in its continuity, and the church theologian in turn acknowledges the relativity of every concrete form compared with the exclusive absoluteness of the religious principle itself.

The cultural-theological ideal itself, however, goes farther than the distinction between cultural theology and ecclesiastical theology. Yet it does not demand a culture that eliminates the distinction drawn between the profane or secular pole and the holy, for that is impossible in the world of reflection and abstraction, but it does demand one in which the entire cultural movement is filled by a homogeneous substance, a directly spiritual material, which turns it into the expression of an all-embracing religious spirit whose continuity is one with that of culture itself. In that case, the opposition of cultural theology and church theology is eliminated, for it is only the expression of a split between substance and meaning in culture.

Even in a new, unified culture, however, the task of working on the predominately religious-cultural elements would be entrusted to the theologian, with the idea of producing a specifically religious community that would not differ in reality from the rest of the cultural community. Instead, and precisely in the manner of the pietistic communities in the seventeenth century, which liked to refer to themselves as *ecclesiola in ecclesia,* the church, as far as theology of culture is concerned, will be something like an *ecclesiola in ecclesia* to the cultural community as such. The church is the circle, as it were, to which is assigned—ideally speaking—the task of creating a specifically religious sphere and thus removing the element of contingency from the living religious elements, collecting them, concentrating them in theory and in practice, and in this way making them into a powerful—indeed, into the most powerful—cultural factor, capable of supporting everything else.

Let me add a few closing words on the subject of the most important supporters of cultural-theological work, that is, the theological faculties. What is the meaning of the theological faculties, and what significance do they possess in this particular connection? The theological faculties are regarded by science with suspicion, and rightly so, in two cases. First, when theology is defined as a scientific knowledge of God in the sense of one particular object among others. Second, when theology is taken to mean a description of a definite and limited denomination with authoritarian claims. In both instances the autonomy of other functions is threatened, even if outwardly they still seem to run independently side by side. A *universitas litterarum,* considered in terms of systematic unity, is then not possible. These objections at once disappear when theology is defined as a normative branch of knowledge concerned with religion and put on the same level as normative ethics, aesthetics, etc. The meaning of "standpoint" in the cultural branches of knowledge must be made clear at the same time, as was done at the beginning of this lecture. Regarded from the standpoint of theology of culture, however, the theological faculties are not only entitled to the same rights as others, but acquire, as do the purely philosophical faculties also, a universal and outstandingly high cultural significance. The theological faculties then perform one of the greatest and most creative tasks within the scope of culture. The demand for the removal of the theological faculties originated in the age of liberalism and of individualistic and antithetical culture. Socialism, by reason of its enmity toward the existing churches, unhesitatingly took up this demand for removal; although the demand contradicts the nature of socialism, for its nature is that of a cultural unity. It must be admitted that socialism has no room for a hierarchy or theocracy or heteronomy of the religious, but in order to complete its own development it needs the all-embracing religious substance which through theonomy alone can free the autonomy of the individual and also that of the individual cultural function from their self-destroying isolation. For this reason we need theological faculties for the new, unifying culture springing from socialist soil; and the first and fundamental task of these faculties is a theology of culture. For nearly two hundred years theology has been in the unfortunate but unavoidable situation of a defender whose position is finally untenable and who is forced to relinquish point after point, and now must again take the offensive, after abandoning the last trace of its untenable, culturally heteronomous position. It must fight under the banner of theonomy, and under this banner it will conquer, not the autonomy of culture but the profanation, exhaustion, and disintegration of culture in the latest epoch of mankind. It will conquer because, as Hegel says, religion is the beginning and the end of all things, and also the center, giving life and soul and spirit to all things.

Index